Management and Administration of the School Library Media Program

by

DOROTHY T. TAGGART

Library Professional Publications
1980

© Dorothy T. Taggart

First published 1980 as a

Library Professional Publication

an imprint of The Shoe String Press, Inc.

Hamden, Connecticut 06514

Printed in the United States of America

Library of Congress Cataloging in Publication Data
Taggart, Dorothy T   1917-
    Management and administration of the school library media program.

    Bibliography: p.
    Includes index.
    1.   School libraries—Administration.   2.   Instruc-
tional materials centers—Administration.   I.   Title.
Z675.S3T117   027.8   80-21052
ISBN 0-208-01853-0
ISBN 0-208-01848-4 (pbk.)

Contents

Foreword

During the decade from 1965 to 1975 the term, *library media center*, came to mean a place in an individual school or attendance center where resources for learning were organized systematically to provide easy accessibility for students and teachers. These centers began to include a wide variety of book and nonbook materials, necessary equipment, an ample budget for activities, a differentiated staff to encourage optimum utilization of all resources, and space enough to permit full program development.

This "combination of resources that includes people, materials, machines, facilities and environments" promotes the intellectual, cultural, social, and ethical development of both faculty and students. Under the skillful direction of trained library media specialists, such as the author, exemplary library media programs have been developed to demonstrate positive contributions to the educational program.

Mrs. Dorothy Taggart has worked effectively with teachers and administrators in her own school district, with leaders in the library media profession, and with community groups in planning and developing a comprehensive program of learning resources for her school district, community, and state. This book has a unique contribution to make in program planning wherever this concept of a unified library and audiovisual program is adopted. It explains the operation of a school media program which embraces instruction, service, and learning activities throughout the school. Such a program expands far beyond the four walls of traditional library quarters and en-

riches all phases of the school program by means of its personnel, materials, and equipment.

With a full realization of its potentials a media program such
as the one described insures both individualized quality formal
education during the school years, and preparation of each
student for a lifetime of continuing learning and self fulfillment.

MONA ALEXANDER
Education Media Specialist
Library Media
Kansas State Department of
Education

Preface

The library media field is a rapidly changing and expanding one with many possibilities for innovative approaches to instructional problems and opportunities. The creative media specialist has the opportunity to build a program which is the center and an intrinsic part of the educational program of the school. This book is intended as a source book and guide for the media specialist, one which will answer questions, give solutions to problems, and provide general basic information. Its focus is on the library media center in the individual school building and quite specifically upon the varied aspects of management and administration. The management and administrative functions of the media specialist involve the decision-making process, budgeting and accounting, staff development and training, evaluation of program, and relationships with school management and the community.

Media administration in the school is changing rapidly with the emphases on program and services to the user, teacher or student, rather than on the technical processes of library operation. There is particular emphasis on evaluative criteria and procedures since they are the basis of any successful new development in the media field.

The attempt has been to make the book practical; it is planned to help the inexperienced media specialist as well as to give the experienced practitioner innovative ideas. The library media field is a challenging one with great variety and new possibilities of better program and service through improvement of management and administrative techniques.

10

MANAGEMENT AND ADMINISTRATION

The author has visited library media centers in many areas of the country, including Washington state, Florida, Colorado, Michigan, Minnesota, Connecticut, and other New England States, as well as many in the Middle West. She has engaged in advanced study in the school library field, and workshops in media use and administration; she teaches media administration at the university level in addition to her job as director of the library media center in a secondary school in Kansas which has served as a demonstration library for the state.

Interlibrary cooperation in Kansas is in the direction of wider use of present collections through all types of libraries working together. Pilot projects include one in cataloging which makes a unified catalog and materials in the audiovisual field available to all libraries and library media centers in Central Kansas. Another interlibrary project, a pilot project for Kansas, is direct-dial, teleprinter-to-teleprinter access service with high school, university and college, and public libraries participating. The third, a Right-to-Read project, is a staff improvement project with forty faculty members participating. The author was codirector of a district-wide curriculum study, a Five-Year Master Plan for Education, one of seven funded in the state, and directed or was actually involved in the other efforts in interlibrary cooperation.

Grateful acknowledgment is made to all those who assisted in the development of this book: the media specialists who presented projects to discuss and ideas to consider; those who have shown their library media centers and described their techniques; and the many leaders in Kansas and the nation who have contributed their insights and experiences. They have all helped me to try to fill a need for a precise guide to better service and program in our schools through better organization, professional administration and management, and wise direction of media resources, based on the standards, *Media Programs: District and School,* published in 1975 by the American Library Association and Association for Educational Communications and Technology.

DOROTHY T. TAGGART

I

Relationships with School Management
and The Community

The library media specialist today must demonstrate that
services to media program users support educational development. Public recognition of this fact must be coupled with understanding of financial as well as educational benefit. We must
communicate wisely and well not only with professional colleagues but with the public community of parents and taxpay-
ers and with the student body. The very real responsibility of
the media specialist in this matter must be assumed with all se-
riousness. Financial support for many of our library media
center programs has held up reasonably well but this may not
be true in the future. An organized and sustained effort to develop public understanding and support for our media development programs is vital.

The Climate for Public Support

The efforts of the media director to develop good public relations will be greatly enhanced by a well-organized and coordinated educational program in the school as a whole. Good-
will, understanding, concern on the part of the community,
interest and support, may have been already engendered by
the school. In such a fortunate situation, the media specialist

can improve on an already good situation by keeping channels open, contributing and adding to it. However, if the opposite is true and there is no favorable public relations environment, steps must be taken to create a climate in which to highlight the role of the library media program in the school.

First, last, and most important of all is that the goals, objectives and *purposes* of the school library media program be stated clearly, widely disseminated and thoroughly understood and subscribed to both internally, by those who compose the school community, and externally, by the wider community made up of parents, members of clubs and organizations, owners and workers in local businesses—in short, the voters and supporters who keep the schools in business. If all of these people, and the political leaders and officials who represent them do not fully realize what the school library media program is about, why it is so important to students' learning now, and to the well being of the community now and *later*—when those students will be running the community—it is very difficult to inform them of what a good job you are doing in achieving the purposes and meeting the objectives.

So the very first step must be to formulate, if this has not already been done, or to revise or update, the overarching goals of the school library media program, and to rethink and re-shape the objectives toward achievement of those goals. Everyone needs to know that the school library media program's central concern and business is:

to help teachers individualize instruction and learning opportunities;

to help students learn to analyze, interpret, evaluate, extrapolate, synthesize, read, think, reflect, speak and listen clearly, among many other skills;

to enable students to learn *how to learn* so that they may embark on a lifetime of learning to keep current, competent and confident during a lifetime in which their jobs and careers will often shift and change;

to provide choices, alternatives and motivation that will help students to become self-propelled and independent inquirers capable of making intelligent decisions, of solving problems, and of moving society ahead instead of allowing it to slide backwards.

Plan for Action

This cannot be done by the media specialist alone. It must be accomplished by working with the school administration and its staff of teachers to develop good communication skills and techniques with which to convey the purposes, methods, and objectives of the entire school system, and all of its units and programs, including those of the library media centers in each building. The media specialist has the responsibility of developing good communications within the school and with other libraries in the area.[1] The media specialist must recognize the problems of complementary services—those of the public libraries, for example, and contribute to the betterment of problem areas. Coordination between the special interests of the library media center and the interests of other areas of the school program must be achieved. The director of library media services must analyze the entire information-education resource of the community before a plan of action is formulated. Those forces must be identified and utilized so that collectively, and in good balance, they lead to the accomplishment of established goals. Such is the basis of good public relations in the school and community.

Bases for Promoting and Understanding of the Program

Cooperation and financial support are apt to be greatest where many people, laymen as well as professional, have a knowledge of and involvement in media-use plans and programs. Sharing in planning and decision making is one of the best ways for the layman to gain knowledge and to develop understanding of the program, its problems, and importance to the school. A statement from the American Association of School Administrators says that "to be sensitive to and solicitous of these needs is an initial kind of respect to pay to an individual or to a public."[2]

Basically, the school media specialist must understand that if he* wants someone to support his program, he must be sure

*Please note that the masculine form used throughout is to be taken to mean either male or female, bypassing the awkwardness of "he/she" etc.

that that someone understands its values in relation to the needs of students and teachers; has shared directly or indirectly in planning and development of that program; and has respect for the media specialist as a person and as a professional librarian and manager!

Internal Relations

If it is doing its job, the library media program should directly or indirectly affect the entire school program. It should be at the center of the instructional program, assisting teachers to plan teaching units, to seek resources and advice on materials for classroom use, and to individualize the curriculum to fit the special needs and abilities of all students. Representatives from all the disciplines should be invited and encouraged to participate in the evaluation and planning of the library media center's role in the total instructional program. New programs, new collections, new equipment, new additions to present collections, new uses of the media center should all be planned with staff members.

As the media director works closely with the administrator or superintendent he has won the support of those individuals by such things as complete and accurate records, professional communications to the administration, a businesslike approach to problems and procedures, and, in general, a total professionalism. This understanding and communication will also be effective with the board of education. Direct services to these members is a good means of communications—a demonstration of what can be done in the library media center, whether it is preparation of reference materials, an audiovisual presentation, a collection of current periodical articles brought to the attention of the board or its members. Such means of communication reach into the community and demonstrate the value of good media service—a powerful means of gaining support.

An important asset to the director of library media services, whether on a school or district level, is his opportunity to become widely known among staff members. The media specialist should be recognized for initiative, for leadership in sound professional action; without this success is limited.

The media specialist must enlist the help of teaching and administrative colleagues to create awareness of library media services. They will hopefully inform the library when there is an opportunity for public relations efforts, such as programs, preparation of television scripts, slide shows, or service on committees. In many ways the media specialist can establish good public relations while working with the staff. A record of friendly, capable, industrious, and efficient professional service is one of the surest ways to establish the good will of colleagues.

Specific Steps to Good Public Relations

Keep the administration, the teaching staff, and the board of education informed with interesting information concerning the library media center. A periodic newsletter is recommended for the school and system administration.

Inform the news media in the area of newsworthy items and events in which the library media center is involved; submit copy for the school newspaper and request that a reporter be assigned to the library media center. The copy may include information on new materials in the library media center, student interviews, unusual happenings, or reports of services performed by the media center, in support of school clubs or special projects.

Become involved in community activities, including a Parent Teacher Association, a Book Fair at the public library, a display of ideas for Christmas giving (4-H Christmas Project Program); participate in curriculum and community programs related to the school; accept invitations to speak about the library media center program; invite commercial and social or study groups and clubs to visit and view or use the facilities and collections.

Exchange ideas for utilizing the nationwide focus programs such as Book Week or National Library Week, to highlight the value of local library information resources. Cooperation with other agencies in the community, particularly the public library, is most important. Exchange lists of magazine holdings, 16mm film collections, filmstrips; better yet, a union catalog of these audiovisual materials to include all types and all collections in the area is most valuable.

Make necessary arrangements for student use of the public library, the nearby university library, local museums, planetariums, historical societies, and the like.

Provide consultative services to individuals and community groups; accept invitations to participate in programs.

Within the school a good display area or bulletin board is an effective advertising device.

Guidelines for Better Bulletin Boards or Display Areas

Make displays dramatic and uncluttered for maximum eye appeal.

Use catchy captions; adapt modern advertising techniques.

Be sure displays and exhibits are purposeful, informative, instructive, and attractive.

Avoid a profusion of book jackets.

Use color to advantage.

Change displays frequently.

Consult the art department and students for ideas and advice.

Ask students to plan and arrange displays.

Use a variety of materials, such as cloth of different textures, wallpaper, pictures, maps, corrugated paper, pipe cleaners, three-dimensional objects, mobiles, models, or anything else to provide interest.

Be sure lettering is distinct and large enough to read.

Highlight themes related to birthdays of famous people, special celebrations, seasonal events, hobbies of students and teachers, school events.

Three times a year the Children's Book Council publishes *The Calendar* which is full of ideas to celebrate a variety of events. It also lists booklets and bibliographies which are available.

Poster House and Giant Photos sell a wide variety of decorative and educational posters for children, as well as travel and sport posters.

Other sources are:

U.S. Government Printing Office: maps, pictures, posters, pamphlets.

Upstart Library Promotionals, Box 889, Hagerstown, MD 21740

See the "Checklist" of each issue of *Library Journal*. Many posters, pamphlets, and bibliographies are available.

See the checklist or similar section of other library media publications.

Examples of Good Public Relations Programs

In Mountain View Intermediate School District No. 48, in Beaverton, Oregon, where the school population numbers 967 children and the staff in the media program consists of two professionals, two support persons and two volunteer persons, one of the support positions is that of a Community Resource Coordinator. This position was created by teacher demand and helps the staff know the resources of the community. The Coordinator may help locate guest speakers and people who have special talents and abilities which could enrich learning; acts as liaison for volunteer activities in the building; and brings services to the building level where they are most satisfactory. Such services are related specifically to the needs of the individual building. The concept that the school library media program, if effective, is a community information program and should draw upon the resources of the entire community as well as print and nonprint material, is basic to this concept in Beaverton. This key support position has spurred the growth of a powerful media program within the school.

The second support person in Beaverton Mountain View Intermediate School working under the auspices of the library media center program is an Independent Study Facilitator. The Facilitator works directly with students who come to the media center to study. An observer states, "This is the one who keeps the kids on task when they come into the media center. This makes for good public relations for the media center, as well as freeing the media specialist to work with teachers in instruction and curriculum development."[3]

In Wellington, Kansas, Unified School District 353, the media specialist at the senior high school has served with the assistant superintendent of schools as codirector of several federally funded projects within the district. The extensive curriculum study in schools serving 2,200 students was funded by the state of Kansas as a pilot project, a Five-Year Master Education Program. An advisory committee composed principally of lay persons together with students and staff meet regularly throughout the school year with departmental teachers to discuss and learn more about what is being taught. The resulting curriculum document is a master plan for the curriculum with goals, objectives, self-evaluation, and program.

In the words of the consultant to the program, Dr. R. Larry Roberts, East High School Principal, Wichita: "Seldom does a school system and its community grasp the opportunity to both evaluate their present position and develop futuristic goals and aspirations on a district-wide basis. Such a program was developed by the Wellington schools in a systematic long-range planning and evaluation program. Supportive data included extensive questionnaires to the public, to students and to faculty. There has been thorough examination of goals, methodologies and techniques for each area of the curriculum. The educational staff has developed a long-range plan using their professional expertise to provide leadership and accountability. Additionally, the development of a long-range plan allows for ease of reevaluation and adjustment or modification based upon everchanging environmental factors.

The entire Wellington community is to be commended for its activities and can take justifiable pride in the results of their arduous labor. Their cooperative spirit will surely be manifested in a more dynamic and relevant educational environment for the young people of Unified School District 353, Wellington, Kansas."[4]

Another innovative program in Kansas which has brought public interest and support of the library media center in the school is that of the South Central Kansas Library System Interlibrary Cooperation Project in which three high schools, the Associated Colleges of Central Kansas (seven campuses and their libraries), and sixty-five public libraries of the South Central Kansas Library System participated. Community colleges in the area also participated. Five teleprinter-to-teleprinter installations served the system, with the regional library serving as the network center. This was a pilot project to test the effectiveness and use of such interlibrary cooperation. Loan requests were placed on the statewide Kansas Information Circuit, the Denver Bibliographic Center, and the Ohio College Library Center (OCLC) search systems. The project was successful, as supported by statistics, in terms of the development of a process for active service communications among a group of school, academic, and public libraries. Public use within the community of one participating high school was overwhelming; patrons of the school district found the TWX access to a wide collection of media most attractive and useful. It was a good means of improving and increasing public relations within the community and school.[5]

Conclusion

Quality library programs must be a part of the school if that school is to meet today's educational goals. The library media specialist and the library media center must have a prime role in developing school relationships with the community and good internal public relations within the school.

The library media center with its human and physical resources is uniquely equipped in today's school to build on and to foster the interest and enthusiasm of the learner and to stimulate new interests and new enthusiasms. The library media center can lead the way in changing the focus from teaching to learning. It is the best place to learn how to learn: the availability of materials, the flexible accessible facilities, the guidance of the media specialist, and the individual motivation of the student can interact here. Here the young person can develop both a source of his need for information and satisfaction in fulfilling that need, which can become lifelong.

But no matter how excellent the program and services of the

library media center, the public inadequately understands them. There may not be, and often is not, an understanding of the differences between the capabilities of professionals and other library workers, or of the surprising variety of services which the library media center has to offer. "To reach an ill-informed public we have traditionally turned to beefed-up public relations efforts, usually in terms of spending more money to publicize existing programs. We need better ways to communicate with citizens."[6]

Notes

1. Erickson, Carlton W. H. *Administering Instructional Media Programs* (New York: Macmillan, 1968), p. 586.
2. *Public Relations for American Schools.* 28th Yearbook of the American Association of School Administrators of the N.E.A. (Washington, D.C.: National Education Association, 1950), p. 29.
3. Baker, D. Philip. *School and Public Library Media Programs for Children and Young Adults.* (Syracuse, New York: Gaylord Professional Publications, 1977), pp. 277–278.
4. *Master Education Program, Unified School District 353.* (Wellington, Kansas: U.S.D. 353, 1978), pp. i, ii.
5. Taggart, Dorothy T. "Innovative Programs in Kansas Media Centers," *Audiovisual Instruction* 22 (November 1977): 22–23.
6. Berry, John. "Discovering the Public," *Library Journal* 102 (September 15, 1977): 1799.

For Further Reading

Aborn, C. M. "Azalea Middle School: The Selling of a Media Program." *Florida Media Quarterly* vol. 2, no. 3, pp. 8–11.
Angoff, A., ed. *Public Relations for Libraries: Essays in Communication Techniques.* Westport, Conn.: Greenwood Press, 1973.
Barber, P. "Public Relations." In American Library Association, ALA Yearbook 1977, 260–3. Chicago: American Library Association, 1977.
Barry, A. "School Library Public Relations Program: What We

Do and How We Do It." *Ohio Association of School Librarians Bulletin,* 27 (January 1975): 7–10.

Berry, J. N. "Selling of the Library." *Library Journal,* 99 (January 15, 1974).

Baughman, Dale. "Yardsticks for Measuring School-Community Relations." *Educational Administration and Supervision* 43 (1957): 19–22.

Bortner, Doyle M. *Public Relations for Teachers.* New York: Simmons-Boardman Publishing, 1959.

Brown, James W., and others. *Administering Educational Media: Instructional Technology and Library Services.* 2nd ed. New York: McGraw-Hill, 1972.

Brown, M. Ruth. "Ring the Bells and Let the People Know." *Audiovisual Instruction* 2, (January 1957): 10–11.

Brownell, Clifford Lee; Gans, Leo; and Maroon, Tufie Z. *Public Relations in Education.* New York: McGraw-Hill, 1955.

Carney, D., and Pendergraft, W. "Media Man: Or Why, Succeeding in Show Business is Really Trying." *North Carolina Libraries* 34, (Winter 1977): 60–61.

Dapper, Gloria. *Public Relations for Education.* New York: Macmillan, 1964.

Darling, M. "School Public Relations Workshop." *New Jersey Libraries* 9 (September 1976): 7.

Davies, Ruth Ann. *The School Library: A Force for Educational Excellence.* New York: Bowker, 1969.

Edmunds, V. "Media of Public Relations." *Ohio Media Spectrum* 29 (May 1977): 4–6.

Erickson, Carlton W. H. *Administering Instructional Media Programs.* New York: Macmillan, 1968.

Foskett, John M. "New Facts about Lay Participation." *Nations Schools* 54 (August 1954): 63–66.

Gaver, Mary V. *Services of Secondary School Media Centers: Evaluation and Development.* Chicago: American Library Association, 1971.

Good Public Relations. In Freeman, P. *Pathfinder: An Operational Guide for the School Librarian,* pp. 156–80. New York: Harper & Row, 1975.

Govan, James F. "The Better Mousetrap: External Accountability and Staff Participation." *Library Trends,* Fall 1977.

Griffith, R. L. "Library Sampling: Program to Inform Young Patrons About the Services in the Children's and Junior High Departments." *Library Journal* 99 (November 1974): 3024.

Hallworth, F. *Publicity and Promotion.* (In *Manual of Library Economy.*) Shoe String, Bingley, C. 1977, pp. 371–85.

Hoehn, T. *Public Relations Ideas for Your Library: For Librarians and Learning Center Directors.* Galesburg, Ill.: Log City Books, 1974.

"Isn't It Good to Know? Library PR That Works." *American Libraries* 6 (May 1975): 285–6.

Kies, C. N. *Problems in Library Public Relations.* New York: Bowker, 1974.

Kindred, Leslie W. *How To Tell the School Story.* Englewood Cliffs, N.J.: Prentice-Hall, 1960.

Laughlin, M. "Action Activities: A Program of PR." *Learning Today* 9 (Summer-Fall 1976): 90–92.

Luster, A. D. C. "Tribute to John and Mary: Winning the John Cotton Dana Public Relations Awards Contest." *Hawaii Library Association Journal* 30 (December 1973): 3–10.

McCloskey, Gordon. *Education and Public Understanding.* New York: Harper & Row, 1959.

Marchant, M. P. "Public Relations and Library Power." *Idaho Libraries* 25 (October 1973): 139–45.

Meyers, J. K. "Passport to Freedom." *Ohio Association of School Librarians Bulletin* 28 (October 1976): 30–31.

Miller, William C. "Winning Staff Support." *Audiovisual Instruction* 2 (October 1957): 206–207.

Moehlman, Arthur B., and van Zwoll, James A. *School Public Relations.* New York: Appleton-Century-Crofts, 1957.

Nelms, W. "Practicing Librarian: Personalizing Service in a Growing Library." *Library Journal* 103 (March 15, 1978): 623.

Olsen, Edward G., ed. *School and Community.* 2nd ed. Englewood Cliffs, N.J.: Prentice-Hall, 1954.

Posmer, M. "P. P." (program planning) and "P. R." (public relations): Two Keys to Circulation Success." *School Library Journal* 22 (February, 1976): 15–19.

Robinson, Edward J. *Communication and Public Relations*. Columbus, Ohio: Charles E. Merrill, 1966.

Rossoff, Martin. *The School Library and Educational Change*. Littleton, Colo.: Libraries Unlimited, 1971.

Simmons, M. L. *Public Relations and the Library*. In American Library Association Intellectual Freedom Manual, pp. 15–20. Chicago: American Library Association, 1974.

Tiffany, Burton C. "Quality Libraries: A Must for Quality Education." *School Media Quarterly*, Fall 1975, pp. 37–42.

Unargo, Daniel. *How to Create a Better Understanding of Our Schools*. Minneapolis: Denison, 1959.

Wezeman, F. "Should a School Library Advertise?" *Journal of Educational Librarianship* 17 (Winter 1977): 188–90.

II

Evaluation of the Program of The Library Media Center

Evaluation is defined as "the process of examining and judging concerning the worth, quality, significance, amount, degree, or conditions of" (Webster's *Third New International Dictionary*).[1] Evaluation of the library media program in the school and its services must be a continuing reappraisal. Educational quality is not permanent nor absolute but is ever changing. The school and its library media center must meet the needs of contemporary society, a relative and changing goal. Educational programs which are excellent must be evaluated and changed continually, as well as those which have far to go in achieving excellence.

Before beginning an evaluation the term *media program* or *library media program* must be defined. Charles W. Adams, writing in *School Media Quarterly* defines media program as: "A media program is the sum total of all the media services originating in a media center or learning activities involving media which are coordinated by the media staff."[2]

Media center programs must reflect changes in educational media and technology, communications theory, and the basic contributions of library and information science research. Today's programs must offer functions, services, and programs to accomplish the purposes of education and the school.

Definition of Terms

Criterion, criteria (pl). A standard, norm, or judgment selected as a basis for quantitative and qualitative comparison.

Evaluative Criteria. (1) The standards against which a person or group or a procedure may be checked; (2) the factors considered by an accrediting agency in analyzing the status of an educational institution to determine whether it shall be accredited.

Evaluative Method. The procedure in a study that has evaluation as its chief purpose and which, in most cases, includes some definite fact-finding, through observation, the careful description of aspects to be evaluated, a statement of purpose, frame of reference, and criteria for the evaluation, and the degrees or terms that are to be employed in recording judgments.

Rating Scale. A device used in evaluating products, attitudes, or other characteristics of instructors or learners.

School Survey. A study or evaluation of a school, a school system, or any part thereof; may be fact-finding, or may indicate the strong and weak features, as judged by definite criteria: *commonly concluded with suggestions for needed changes and/or recommendations for more desirable practices.*

Standard. (1) A goal or objective or criterion of education expressed either numerically as a statistical average or philosophically as an ideal of excellence; (2) any criterion by which things are judged.[3]

The following twelve criteria are identified as being basic for judging excellence, as identified by the American Association of School Administrators and the National School Boards Association.

Evaluation should be based on stated objectives.

Evaluation should be based on intimate and comprehensive knowledge of the community.

Evaluation should be a continuous activity.

Evaluation should be comprehensive.

Evaluation should be a cooperative process involving many people.

Evaluation should identify strengths as well as deficiencies.

Evaluation should involve many measuring instruments.
Evaluation should be based on knowledge of children and
     youth.
Evaluation requires the board to look at itself.
Evaluation should appraise existing practices affecting
     the staff.
Evaluation is based on the belief that what people think
     makes a difference.
Evaluation should culminate in self-improvement.[4]

The leadership in the field of evaluation of secondary
schools has come from *The Cooperative Study of Secondary School
Standards*, now known as *The National Study of Secondary School
Evaluation*. Evaluative instruments formulated by this study
have included:

> *Evaluative Criteria* (Senior High School)[5]
> *Evaluative Criteria for Junior High Schools*[6]

These are the two most used evaluative instruments for secondary schools and provide, in principle, the basis for many
state and local measurement instruments. A listing of such instruments which include evaluation of the school library media
center would be comprised of those from almost every state
and many communities. These are available from the several
state departments of education; those for the state of Kansas
are included, for the purpose of comparison, at the end of this
chapter. In many areas they are either identical or comparable
with the criteria of other states. They do give media specialists
a basis for evaluation of the media program and service.

The North Central Association of Colleges and Secondary
Schools, founded in 1895, has developed criteria for the policies and standards for both the junior and senior high school
which give full attention to school media programs. (These will
be found at the end of this chapter.)

"The purpose of the Association shall be the development
and maintenance of high standards of excellence for universities, colleges, and schools, the continued improvement of the
educational program and the effectiveness of instruction on
secondary and college levels through a scientific and professional approach to the solution of educational problems, the

establishment of cooperative relationships between secondary schools and colleges and universities within the territory of the Association, and the maintenance of effective working relationships with other educational organizations and accrediting agencies." (Articles of Incorporation of the North Central Association).

Other regional associations have similar aims and purposes. The North Central Association of Colleges and Secondary Schools includes nineteen states in the center of the nation. The media specialist in the school of today must be abreast of changes in school administration and evaluation programs, as well as those relating specifically to the library media program.

Schools throughout the nation have at hand a new basis for evaluating the media program in their schools in *Media Programs: District and School* (1975), which looks ahead to the school of the next decade. This publication is a joint effort of the American Association of School Librarians, A.L.A., and the Association for Educational Communications and Technology (since 1971 the AECT, but formerly the Department of Audiovisual Instruction of the National Education Association). This joint effort symbolizes and expresses the intent of formerly book-oriented-only librarians and formerly (for the most part) hardware oriented AV practitioners to work together to sustain and improve school media services at every level in the schools. It reflects the thinking of many professionals in the library media field. The guidelines developed through cooperative effort will, if followed, assist greatly to maintain and evaluate a quality and up to date media program to support the changing educational curricula in the school. Focus is upon qualitative goals (rather than quantities of materials or numbers of staff) and an up to date philosophy of school library media service. Alternative structures and operational choices in achieving goals are presented. The guidelines are intended for use by school administrators, boards of education, school architects, and all others who seek responsible criteria for establishing and evaluating programs.

The greatest contribution, perhaps, of the new guidelines is their emphasis on district leadership and cooperative programs. A continued concern for revision in the future is expressed by both organizations. Both AASL and AECT urge that media professionals, persons in school media programs, and other educational leaders utilize the recommendations to improve the educational opportunities for learning.[7]

The cooperation of the leaders in the library field with those in the audiovisual field has been a growing concept, but the new standards in *Media Programs: District and School* (1975) are the culmination of collaboration begun with the development of the 1969 *Standards.* The growing concept of program, basic to both the 1960 and 1969 *Standards,* has now been explored by both the library and audiovisual field culminating in a philosophy which includes both areas, and emphasizes that the program of the library media center includes all media and materials, as well as equipment and service.

There are a number of guides to programs that are consonant with the recommendations of the nationally devised standards or guidelines. One of the best was issued by the North Carolina State Department of Public Instruction in 1961 to help the development in that state of good programs for the library media center. In 1963, an outstanding report by Ralph Ellsworth was issued for the purpose of presenting new ideas for physical quarters based on the concept of the program which a school requires.[8]

Carlton W. H. Erickson in *Administering Instructional Media Programs* (1968) gave more attention to program than the writings of other audiovisual specialists. It is a helpful analysis of the principles to be followed in developing school media program and services.

Iowa has an excellent guide for development of the library media centers in the state (Iowa, 1969); *The Plan for Progress . . . in the Media Center K-6* is a simple yet explicit plan for building the staff, quarters, facilities, materials collection, professional collection, budget, equipment, and furniture selection for the media program in the elementary school.

What the Media Specialist Should Do

Dr. Frances Henne, a foremost leader and crusader for innovative and excellent library programs in the school, has recommended that "evaluations, whether self-survey or conducted by outside specialists, involve not only the school librarians but also the administration, faculty, and not infrequently, the students and parents." The pattern of having some person or persons "blow in, blow off, and blow out," although not unknown in the annals of school library evaluations, has little to commend it. "Under any circumstances evaluations should be constructive in design and intent, with the primary purpose of working with and assisting the school and the librarians to effect improvements in the library benefiting students and teachers."[9]

The innovative planning guide developed by Frances Henne and her associates in 1951 was one of the first real attempts to base evaluation of the library in the school on an analysis of program.[10] In the more than two decades since this and other publications of Dr. Henne's first appeared, major developments have resulted from the *Standards for the School Library Programs* and from the *Standards for School Media Programs* (American Association of School Librarians, 1960 and 1969) and now from the *Media Programs: District and School* (1975). All of the standards are based on the concept that the quality of the program must determine the nature and amount of quantitative provisions.

Whatever evaluative endeavor may be undertaken by the school, the district, or the state, or even by the individual library media center, the real value of the study lies in the results which come from the findings of evaluation. A plan should be formulated by the media specialist which will list products to come from the evaluative study. Specific programs must be related to instructional program changes, renovations, and innovations. Problem-solving ability is a key characteristic of the successful media specialist. He must find an answer which works well for specific problems and innovations, in order to adapt the library media center's program to the program of the school.

Priorities of the media program, operational as well as philosophical, must be identified and stated when evaluation is considered. Operational priorities must be in order if philosophical priorities are to be met. If meeting user needs successfully is to be the goal of the media program, then all program elements and activities must be evaluated accordingly. What

are the essential components for meeting needs in this particular school at this particular time? Should there be better guidance in the use of media-reading materials, audio or visual?
Should reference services to students be improved? Planning
with teachers? Should assistance by the media staff in production of materials include graphic and transparency production,
as well as off-the-air videotaping? Whatever the operational
objectives of the library media center, their development must
involve teachers, students, and the media staff, and the evaluation of the media center's success in achieving them must also
be a cooperative endeavor.

Evaluation should extend to the degree of coordination between the work of the individual media center and the district,
the media center and the staff of the school, of the professional library with the media center in services to the staff. It
should examine also the smoothness, timeliness, and efficiency
of acquisition and processing services.

Self-evaluation and evaluation by others of the director and
the professional staff must be an area of that evaluation. Criteria for evaluation of the media specialist are in many ways
the same as those for the excellent teacher in the classroom,
but with some significant differences: the media specialist must
manage more money, more people, more conflicting objectives
than any classroom teacher. The quality of the media specialist
is the key to quality of the media center.

Assessment or evaluation in the library media center with a
small staff and in the district without a media coordinator must
come from the media specialist in the school. It is a supervisory
role that must be assumed by the media specialist with the consultation of the state and federal library and education departments. Advice may come from the coordinator in the larger
city system nearby, from the state consultant for library services, or from the staff of the library school where the media
specialist has studied or is studying. It is a basic task. Excellent
sources to consult are found in the section For Further Reading at the end of this chapter.

Basic questions need to be asked by the media specialist, by
the staff of the school, by the administrator, and by all cooperating media centers. Such questions may include:

Is the library media center in the school adequately
    equipped?
Is the media specialist a well-qualified one?
Is the in-service program of development for the entire
    staff good?
How does the school population view the media pro-
    gram? The community?
Are teachers competent in using educational media and
    technology?
Is the collection adequate for the instructional program?
Is the program and service of the center adequate?
    Superior?
What is most important to the success of the program of
    the media center?
Are the objectives and priorities of the center clear? Gen-
    erally supported?
Do they derive from standards and goals which the teach-
    ers, the administrators, the students and the parents
    have had a hand in shaping *with* the library media spe-
    cialist and staff?

We are accustomed to thinking of "input" standards for the
quality and quantity of those elements and resources which
make a quality program possible: money, materials, personnel
and space. We must also train ourselves to think, for evaluation
purposes, of production and process criteria and standards,
and objectives to be stated in terms of them as applied to students, to teachers, the administration, the instructional program, and also the community. Are teachers competent in using instructional media? Teacher competence, and confidence
in trying new methods and in utilizing a greater variety of materials, can and should be one of our most important goals.
Objectives toward fulfillment of this goal can be stated in such
a way as to allow us to evaluate progress toward it. Do students
display an ability to pursue independent research projects?
Surely, a high standard of excellence in this regard must mark
any school library media program worthy of the name, and
such a product standard can be shaped into a measurable objective exactly tailored to a particular school and its students.

The very first of the twelve criteria for judging excellence as identified by the American Association of School Administrators and the National School Boards Association, was, you will recall, "Evaluation should be based on stated objectives." This is of such importance that it can hardly be overemphasized, and must be kept constantly in mind in setting up evaluation procedures for the school library media program. Without measurable objectives, and without the standards of expected performance to back them up, evaluation cannot really be meaningful, or a valid part of the feedback, self-improvement, continuous quality control loop.

In the development of criteria for the local library media center evaluation, standards of reference or criteria must be stated in definite and succinct language. Higher goals than those found in the present program should be formulated and be a part of the preparation of written plans and proposals. There is always room for improvement. Standards of excellence on the part of the media specialist and teachers must be defined in terms of valid curriculum planning and professional excellence.

Careful consideration should be given to the problem of symbols of judgment when measuring instruments are constructed. Evaluation forms should be arranged for quick and easy responses whenever possible. In some cases, teachers will reveal deeper insight when asked to write out answers to questions. The following symbols of status and change are commonly used:

1. yes and no.
2. satisfactory and unsatisfactory.
3. condition 1 (missing), condition 2 (poor), condition 3 (fair), condition 4 (good), condition 5 (excellent).
4. 5—very superior, 4—superior, 3—average, 2—inferior, 1—very inferior.
5. great deal, some and very little.
6. 1—constantly, 2—periodically, 3—seldom, 4—never.
7. + (Condition is present or satisfactory), − (Condition is fairly or poorly met), 0 (Condition not met, or unsatisfactory. N (Not applicable to the situation).

8. Slightly, Moderately, Excellent.
9. Poor, Fair, Good, Very Good, Excellent.[11]

The time of the evaluation provides the unique climate for change. The opportunity should never be allowed to pass. Evaluation leads naturally into the process of: (1) summarization and generalization of the evidence; (2) reporting results interestingly to the staff in written and graphic form by bulletins; (3) suggesting study of results prior to sectional, school, or committee meetings; (4) holding a series of analysis and planning meetings where some significant problems may be listed in priority for consideration; (5) ascertaining in those meetings the underlying causes for weak conditions and *formulating a set of recommendations for action and improvement.*[12]

The following are examples of state and regional standards:

BULLETIN 301

Rules, Regulations, Standards,
And Procedures for Accrediting
Elementary Schools.

Filed January 1, 1975
Effective September 1, 1975.
Kansas State Department of Education.

91–4–6 STANDARD VI—LIBRARY MEDIA CENTER.

A. DISTRICT LIBRARY MEDIA PROGRAM.
   1. The district library media program shall be organized to:
      a. Include the entire district or a consortium of districts when utilizing personnel, services, materials and equipment.
      b. Provide in-service programs in the use of library media and equipment.
   2. The district library media program shall be implemented by:
      a. A written policy statement concerning the selec-

tion and optimum use of library media including procedures for dealing with controversial materials.

   b. Establishing coordinated services for cataloging and processing, maintenance of material and equipment and delivery services.

   c. Providing for an annual evaluation process to determine the effectiveness of the district library media program in relation to the goals and objectives of the total educational program.

   d. Utilizing all available media resources within the district and, if feasible, with surrounding districts, including personnel, materials, and equipment. Public or community resources shall also be utilized whenever possible.

B. SCHOOL LIBRARY MEDIA CENTER PROGRAM.

The library media center program shall be an integral part of the school. It shall provide:

1. A long-range plan formulated by administrators, teachers, library media specialists, and students.
2. Expansion of classroom experiences.
3. Provision for reading, listening, and viewing activities.
4. Continuous evaluation of objectives, services, and media.
5. A written media selection policy.

C. LIBRARY MEDIA CENTER STAFF.

1. The central library media center shall be staffed by a library specialist who holds a certificate valid for teaching in the elementary school and has at least minimum library education (library education and audiovisual courses) of fifteen semester hours. Schools of fewer than 150 pupils may have classroom collections, part-time consultant services of a library media specialist should be available.

D. LIBRARY MEDIA CENTER MATERIALS AND RESOURCES.

1. Each school of 150 or more students shall have a library media center with a well-balanced collection of

books, basic reference materials, periodicals, and nonprint media (audiovisual materials) appropriate to the
objectives of the school and needs of the students and
teachers.

2. Classification and cataloging of the collection shall include a shelf list and an alphabetically arranged catalog with classification by the Dewey Decimal System.

3. Inventory and finance records shall be accurate and
   up to date.

4. Expenditures. After a media program has acquired a
   minimum balanced print and nonprint collection, the
   annual expenditure for books, magazines, and nonprint media (exclusive of textbooks and equipment)
   shall be as follows:
   K–12—$6.00 per student.

E. BOOK COLLECTIONS.

1. Requirements pertaining to number of pupils and
   books per pupil. (See Table I.)

TABLE I

Effective September 1, 1976

Number of Pupils	Books Per Pupil
1 to 75	15 books per pupil
75 to 200	1,125 books plus 6 books for each additional pupil beyond 75
200 to 300	1,875 books plus 4 books per pupil beyond 200
300 to	2,275 books plus 4 books per pupil beyond 300

A school with twelve or fewer pupils enrolled shall spend at
least $30.00 annually for library purposes.

2. Adequacy of Collection—Effective September 1, 1976.

   a. Schools with an enrollment of fewer than 500 students
      shall meet the following requirements:

Effective September 1, 1976	
Number of Pupils	*Books Per Pupil*
1 to 75	20 books per pupil
76 to 200	1,500 books plus 10 books for each additional pupil beyond 75
201 to 500	2,750 books plus 10 books per pupil beyond 200

  b. For schools with enrollments over 500 students the minimum collection shall be ten (10) books per student.

  c. The collection shall also contain a sufficient number of nonprint materials for use in the classroom, in the school library media center and for home use to meet the objectives of the library media center and for home use as given above. If a school maintains an innovative program such as team teaching, modular scheduling, dial access, television, or individualized instruction, more materials will be required.

  d. Selection of all materials for the collection shall be made cooperatively by the library media specialist, teacher, students, parents and administrators.

ALTERNATIVE—STANDARD VI.

As an alternative to the foregoing Standard VI, a school shall have the prerogative to meet the following requirements:

A. Each elementary school shall have a library media center with a well-balanced collection of books, basic reference material, and periodicals and audiovisual materials appropriate to the objectives of the school and needs of the students and teachers. This collection shall provide reading, listening, and viewing materials in all subject areas of the school curriculum. It shall contain basic information as well as enrichment materials.

B. Classification and cataloging of the collection shall include a shelf list and an alphabetically arranged catalog with classification with the Dewey Decimal System.

C. Inventory and finance records shall be accurate and up to date.

D. The central library media center shall be staffed by a librarian or media specialist who holds a certificate valid for teaching in the elementary school and has at least minimum library education (library education and audiovisual courses) of fifteen semester hours.

E. Professional materials for teachers shall include at least five professional magazines dealing with general teaching methods as well as specific areas of organization and use of educational media both printed and audiovisual. Self-instructional materials to help teachers select and use audiovisual materials more effectively may also be included in the collection.

F. The school shall produce in writing the library media plan for the school and shall state specifically the amount of time the staff will be assigned; the collection, both print and nonprint; budget and expenditures; facilities, materials, and equipment that will be utilized in the development of the library media program.

The school shall produce written evidence demonstrating the development of goals and objectives with expected outcomes. The goals and objectives shall be reasonably commensurate and in agreement with state-wide educational goals as adopted by the State Board of Education and with recognized educational concepts and practices, and shall have broad-base community involvement in their formulation. Experimental or innovative programs, also supported by written goals, objectives, and expected outcomes, are encouraged. Goals and objectives shall be developed within a three-year period in three phases. Phase I shall be the establishment of local committees. Phase II shall cover the writing of goals and objectives with expected outcomes. Phase III shall include the implementation of the goals and objectives throughout the school and/or district.

Also, such plan shall indicate the amount and kinds of supportive services available to the school that supplement the library media program of the school.

Such library media plan shall be approved by the local board of education and be on file with the clerk of the board and copies shall be provided for each administrator and for each library media specialist in the school.

The library media plan shall be approved by the State Department of Education and shall be placed on file with the State Department of Education.

(Authorized by K.S.A. 1968 Supp. 72–7513; K.S.A. 1968 Supp. 72–7514; Effective January 1, 1970; amended January 1, 1972; amended January 1, 1973; Amended January 1, 1974).

BULLETIN 101

Rules, Regulations, Standards, and Procedures for Accrediting Junior High Schools.
Filed January 1, 1975.   Effective September 1, 1975.

Kansas State Department of Education, Kansas State Education Building, 120 East 10th Street, Topeka, Kansas.

91–3–7   STANDARD VII—LIBRARY MEDIA CENTER.

A. DISTRICT LIBRARY MEDIA PROGRAM.
  1. The district library media program shall be organized to:
      a. Include the entire district or a consortium of districts when utilizing personnel, services, materials, and equipment.
      b. Provide in-service programs in the use of library media and equipment.

  2. The district library media program shall be implemented by:

    a. A written policy statement concerning the selection and optimum use of library media including procedures for dealing with controversial materials.
    b. Establishing coordinating services for cataloging and processing, maintenance of material and equipment, and delivery services.
    c. Providing for an annual evaluation process to determine the effectiveness of the district library media program in relation to the goals and objectives of the total educational program.
    d. Utilizing all available media resources with the district and, if feasible, with surrounding districts, including personnel, materials, and equipment. Public or community resources shall be utilized whenever possible.

B. SCHOOL LIBRARY MEDIA CENTER PROGRAM.
The library media center program shall be an integral part of the total program of the school. It shall provide:
1. A long-range plan formulated by administrators, teachers, library media specialists, and students.
2. Expansion of classroom experiences.
3. Provision for reading, listening, and viewing activities.
4. Continuous evaluation of objectives, services, and media.
5. A written media selection policy.

C. LIBRARY MEDIA CENTER STAFF.
1. The library media specialist shall hold a Kansas teacher certificate valid on the level at which he serves and shall meet the preparation requirements as indicated by E.

D. LIBRARY MEDIA MATERIALS AND RESOURCES.
1. Each school shall have a library media center with a well-balanced collection of books, basic reference material, periodicals, and nonprint media (audiovisual materials) appropriate to the objectives of the school and needs of the students and teachers.

   2. Classification and cataloging of the collection shall in-
      clude a shelf list and an alphabetically arranged cata-
      log with classification by the Dewey Decimal System.
   3. Inventory and finance records shall be accurate and
      up to date.
   4. Expenditures. After a media program has acquired a
      minimum balanced print and nonprint collection, the
      annual expenditure for books, magazines, and non-
      print media (exclusive of textbooks and equipment)
      shall be as follows:
         K–12—$6.00 per student

E. BOOK COLLECTIONS
   1. Requirements pertaining to number of pupils and
      books per pupil. (See Table I.)

BULLETIN 201

Rules, Regulations, Standards
and Procedures for Accrediting
High Schools

Filed January 1, 1975
Effective September 1, 1975

Kansas State Department of Education
Kansas State Education Building
120 East 10th Street
Topeka, Kansas 66612

91–2–7   STANDARD VII—LIBRARY MEDIA CENTER

A. DISTRICT LIBRARY MEDIA PROGRAM
   1. The district library media program shall be organized
      to:
      a. Include the entire district or a consortium of dis-
         tricts when utilizing personnel, services, materials,
         and equipment.

TABLE I

REQUIREMENTS PERTAINING TO SIZE OF SCHOOL, STAFF, PREPARATION OF LIBRARY MEDIA PERSONNEL, AND SIZE OF COLLECTION

Size of School	Professional Staff	Preparation Semester Hours	Collection
Under 100	a. One staff member assigned two 55-minute, or b. Three 40-minute periods each day free of study halls and other supervisory responsibilities.	Fifteen	1,200 volumes
100–199	a. One staff member assigned three 55-minute, or b. Four 40-minute periods each day free of study hall and other supervisory responsibilities.	Fifteen	1,200 volumes for first 120 pupils 10 for additional pupil until enrollment reaches 500.

Table I cont'd

Size of School	Professional Staff	Preparation Semester Hours	Collection
200–499	a. One staff member assigned four 55-minute, or b. Five 40-minute periods each day free of study hall and other supervisory responsibilities.	Fifteen	1,200 volumes for first 120 pupils, 10 for each additional pupil until enrollment reaches 500.
500–799	One or more staff members assigned full time (six clock hours free of study hall and other supervisory responsibilities, plus full-time clerical help.	Twenty-four	5,000 volumes for first 500 pupils, 5 additional books per pupil for next 500 and 3 additional books per pupil over 1,000 pupils enrolled.
800–1,499	Same as above	Same	Same as above
1,500—over	Two full-time staff members plus one full-time clerical help.	Same	Same as above

      b. Provide in-service programs in the use of library media equipment.

  2. The district library media program shall be implemented by:

      a. A written policy statement concerning the selection and optimum use of library media including procedures for dealing with controversial materials.

      b. Establishing coordinated services for cataloging and processing, maintenance of material and equipment, and delivery services.

      c. Providing for an annual evaluation process to determine the effectiveness of the district library media program in relation to the goals and objectives of the total educational program.

      d. Utilizing all available media resources within the district and, if feasible, with surrounding districts, or community resources shall be utilized whenever possible.

B. SCHOOL LIBRARY MEDIA CENTER PROGRAM.

The library media center program shall be an integral part of the total program of the school. It shall provide:

1. A long-range plan formulated by administrators, teachers, library media specialists, and students.
2. Expansion of classroom experiences.
3. Provision for reading, listening, and viewing activities.
4. Continuous evaluation of objectives, services, and media.
5. A written media selection policy.

C. LIBRARY MEDIA CENTER MATERIALS AND RESOURCES.

1. Each school shall have a library media center with a well-balanced collection of books, basic reference material, periodicals, and nonprint media (audiovisual materials) appropriate to the objectives of the school and needs of the students and teachers.
2. Classification and cataloging of the collection shall include a shelf list and an alphabetically arranged catalog with a classification by the Dewey Decimal System.

3. Inventory and finance records shall be accurate and up to date.
4. Expenditures. After a media program has acquired a minimum balanced print and nonprint collection, the annual expenditure for books, magazines, and nonprint media (exclusive of textbooks and equipment) shall be as follows:

    K–12—$6.00 per student

D. The library media specialist shall hold a Kansas teacher certificate valid on the level at which he serves and shall meet the preparation requirements as indicated by E.

E. BOOK COLLECTIONS.
    1. Requirements pertaining to number of pupils and books per pupil. (See Table I.)

ALTERNATIVE—STANDARD VII

As an alternative to the foregoing Standard VII, a school has the prerogative to meet the following requirements:

A. A high school shall have a library media center organized as a source center of instructional materials for the entire educational program.

B. Classification and cataloging of the collection shall include a shelf list and an alphabetically arranged catalog with classification by the Dewey Decimal System.

C. Inventory and finance records shall be accurate and up to date.

D. Professional library media personnel shall hold a valid Kansas teacher certificate and meet requirements as defined in 91–1–22–C–11 A Secondary School Librarian, by the current "Certificate Handbook."

E. Professional materials for teachers shall include at least five professional magazines dealing with general teaching methods as well as specific areas of organization and use of educational media, both printed and audiovisual. Self-instructional materials to help teachers select and use audiovisual materials more effectively may also be used in the collection.

F. The school shall produce in writing the library media plan for the school and shall state specifically the amount of time the staff will be assigned; the collection, both print and nonprint; budget and expenditures; facilities, materials, and equipment that will be utilized in the development of the library media center.

The school shall produce written evidence demonstrating the development of goals and objectives with expected outcomes. The goals and objectives shall be reasonably commensurate and in agreement with state-wide educational goals as adopted by the State Board of Education and with recognized educational concepts and practices, and shall have broad-base community involvement in their formulation. Experimental or innovative programs, also supported by written goals, objectives, and expected outcomes, are encouraged. Goals and objectives shall be developed within a three-year period in three phases. Phase I shall be the establishment of local committees. Phase II shall cover the writing of goals and objectives with expected outcomes. Phase III shall include implementation of the goals and objectives throughout the school and/or district.

Also, such plan shall indicate the amount and kinds of supportive services available to the school that supplement the library media center program of the school.

The library media program shall be approved by the local board of education and be on file with the clerk of the board and copies shall be provided for each administrator and for each library media specialist in the school.

The library media plan shall be approved by the State Department of Education and shall be placed on file with the State Department of Education.

(Authorized by K.S.A. 1968 supp. 72–7513; K.S.A. 1968 supp. 72–7514; Effective January 1, 1970; amended January 1, 1972; amended January 1, 1973; amended January 1, 1974).

POLICIES AND STANDARDS FOR THE APPROVAL OF JUNIOR HIGH/MIDDLE SCHOOLS 1974[16]
NORTH CENTRAL ASSOCIATION OF COLLEGES AND SECONDARY SCHOOLS, 1895

Commission on Secondary Schools
5454 South Shore Drive
Chicago, Illinois 60616

9.11　INSTRUCTIONAL MATERIALS CENTER

The junior high or middle school instructional materials center is a resource center for the school's total educational program. Its function is to locate, gather, provide, organize, and coordinate the school's learning resources and devices and to motivate and assist teachers and students in the effective use of these resources. The center is supplied with adequate books and other educational media which meet the varied needs and interests of the students and staff. The center should enable each student to pursue special interests, to receive special assistance, and to gain a positive attitude toward all instructional materials. The instructional materials center affords staff and students opportunity to make effective use of its materials.

9.2　"A" STANDARDS RELATED TO STRUCTURE

9.21　The junior high or middle school *shall* have an instructional materials center of adequate size. It should be furnished with an adequate supply of educational media including books, films, filmstrips, recordings, tapes, slides, transparencies, pictures, maps, globes, charts, programmed instruction, pamphlets, periodicals, newspapers, realia, and other resources for learning as well as an adequate amount of appropriate equipment for utilization of materials.

Adequate fiscal allotments, budget management, personnel competencies, materials availability, equipment utilization, facilities design, and staff training should be capitalized on in the center's program of services.

(Interpretive Note 1 — The function of the instructional materials center *shall* reflect the philosophy of the school. Its effectiveness *shall* be judged on the basis of how it facilitates the type of instructional program in operation.

Adequacy of size in terms of program in student reading stations is interpreted as follows: In schools enrolling up to 1,000 pupils, 8 percent but not less than 40 stations. In school enrolling from 1,000 to 1,999 pupils, 7 percent but not less than 80 stations. In schools enrolling 2,000 or more pupils, 5 percent but not less than 140 stations. In addition, there *shall* be sufficient work space for the technical processing and repair of materials, for conducting business routines, and for storing supplies and equipment. Even though facilities may not allow consolidation of all instructional materials in one location, control and listing of all materials *shall* be in the central instructional materials center.

Interpretive Note — There is a minimum of 1,200 books, exclusive of textbooks, or at least five books per pupil enrolled, whichever is larger, until the school's enrollment reaches 500. At least three additional books *shall* be provided for each pupil above 500.

Interpretive Note 3 — After a media program has acquired a minimum balanced print and nonprint collection, the annual expenditure for books, magazines, and audiovisual materials (exclusive of textbooks) *shall* be as follows:

Enrollment	*Expenditures*
Fewer than 500	$4.00 per pupil
500–999	$2,000 for the first 500 pupils plus $3.50 per pupil above that
1,000–1,999	$3,750 for the first 1000 pupils plus $3.00 per pupil above that
Over 2,000	$6,750 for the first 2000 pupils plus $2.00 per pupil above that

To keep the staff abreast of current curricular trends and research findings, the school system *shall* make available a professional library of books and periodicals.

Interpretive Note 4 — In addition to funds for new acquisitions, the annual instructional materials budget should include, for purchase, rental, and maintenance of other types of educational media, a sum equal to one percent of each year's pupil instructional allotment.)

9.22   The instructional materials center *shall* be administered by personnel professionally trained in school library and audiovisual services, who are certified as teachers. Personnel *shall* meet state standards of preparation.

(Interpretive Note 1 — Each junior high or middle school *shall* employ at least one such professionally trained person. Schools with an enrollment of less than 400 pupils *shall* employ a professional who devotes full time to materials center service. Adult technical assistants classed as clerks and/or paraprofessionals *shall* be provided to permit the director of the materials center to perform professional functions.

Interpretive Note 2 — The school's daily schedule *shall* provide for the staffing of the center throughout the day with well-trained adult specialists, inclusive of librarians, technicians, and clerks, sufficient to provide needed services for the number of students to be accommodated.)

9.23 The instructional materials center should provide areas for reading, listening, viewing, preparation, and individual learning for staff and students, as well as for storage for materials and equipment.

(Interpretive Note — Even though facilities may not allow consolidation of all areas above in one location, their availability should be readily accessible to both students and staff.)

9.24 The instructional materials center should be located as part of the school so as to be readily accessible to both students and staff.

9.25 The school's instructional materials center should coordinate its services, inventory, and acquisitions with those of any supplementary centers provided by the school districts and/or the community.

9.3 *"B" STANDARDS RELATED TO OPERATION AND FUNCTION*

9.31 In-service training programs for students and staff for making effective use of the services of the instructional materials center *shall* be provided.

9.32 The center *shall* be open to students and the staff throughout the school day and at other times as deemed desirable by the local situation.

9.34 Materials in the center should be evaluated annually in terms of recentness, appropriateness, balance, adequacy, and usage.

9.35 The professional staff of the school, working with the instructional materials center staff, should assume a major responsibility in the selection of materials for the center.

9.36 The staff of the center should make available to all professional staff and students a ready access to the listing of all available educational media.

POLICIES AND STANDARDS FOR THE APPROVAL OF SECONDARY SCHOOLS, 1978–1979
NORTH CENTRAL ASSOCIATION OF COLLEGES AND SCHOOLS

Commission on Schools
5454 South Shore Drive
Chicago, Illinois 60615

STANDARD VIII—INSTRUCTIONAL[17]
MEDIA PROGRAM
(LIBRARY, AUDIOVISUAL, AND INSTRUCTIONAL MATERIALS)

A coordinated instructional media program shall be organized so as to make accessible in any location a wide range of media to teachers and students. In addition to receiving, storing, retrieving, and displaying information in all forms, both in a center and at other locations, equipment and personnel shall be available for the production of a wide range of media for students and faculty. The program shall be developed in such a way as to support instruction through appropriate facilities and professionally and technically prepared staff.

8.1 *Adequacy of Collection.* A minimum collection of 2,500 books, exclusive of high school textbooks and appropriate for instruction needs, shall be provided. Minimum collection requirements as enrollments increase are:

ENROLLMENT	VOLUMES REQUIRED
Fewer than 200 2,500	
200–499 2,500	plus 8 books for each student over 200.
500–999 4,900	plus 6 books for each student over 500.
1,000–1,999 7,900	plus 4 books for each student over 1,000.
Over 2,000 11,000	plus 2 books for each student over 2,000.

In addition to the print material collection described above, the faculty and students should have maximum access to film-strips, 8mm films, tape and disc recordings, and slides within the building as well as 16mm films, videotapes, and other more expensive items which may or may not be stored in the building. If a school maintains an innovative program such as team teaching, modular scheduling, dial access, television, or individualized instruction, more materials and personnel will be required.

Newly organized schools will be given a reasonable amount of time to meet the volume requirement of regular member schools.

(Interpretation: Libraries must first meet the minimum collection of books and then may supplement this by bookmobile service.)

8.2 *Instructional Materials Center and Equipment.* The center shall be attractive, easily accessible, well-lighted, appropriately equipped, and shall accommodate the following proportions of the enrollment at reading stations: In schools enrolling up to 1,000 pupils, 8 percent but not less than 40 stations. In schools enrolling from 1,000 to 1,999 pupils, 7 percent but not less than 80 stations. In schools enrolling 2,000 or more pupils, 5 percent but not less than 140 stations. The center shall not be used as a study hall requiring supervision by the professional staff and reducing reading stations to fewer seats than required above. Sufficient work room and storage space required above shall be provided.

(Interpretation: The high school library must be housed in the high school building.)

8.3 *Professional Media Personnel.* Member schools shall employ the equivalent of at least one professionally trained individual. The professional staff shall provide such services as instructing students in the use of the media center, assisting teachers in locating and utilizing resources, and the production of graphic and other materials. In addition, the professional staff should develop a plan for the evaluation and selection of materials utilizing standard lists and the judgments of teaching staff. In order to provide these services, the equivalent of the following numbers of professional media persons (qualified as librarians or audiovisual specialists) are required according to the enrollment categories shown:

ENROLLMENT	QUALIFIED SPECIALISTS REQUIRED
Fewer than 300	At least one half-time specialist.
300–1,499	At least one full-time specialist.
Over 1,500	At least two full-time specialists.

NOTE: In meeting the above standard, a school shall employ at least one qualified librarian on a half-time basis.

8.4 *Media Program Expenditures.* After a media program has acquired a minimum balanced print and nonprint collection, the annual expenditure for books, magazines, and audiovisual materials (exclusive of textbooks) shall be as follows:

ENROLLMENT	*EXPENDITURE*
Fewer than 500	$6.00 per student
500 to 999	$3,000 for the first 500 students, plus $4.00 per student above that
1,000 to 1,999	$5,000 for the first 1,000 students, plus $3.50 per student above that
Above 2,000	$8,500 for the first 2,000 students, plus $2.50 per student above that

To keep the staff abreast of current curricular trends and research findings, the school system shall make available a professional library of books and periodicals.

NOTE: The contributions of federally funded programs may be counted in meeting this standard.

8.5 *Clerical Help.* In order to permit media specialists to perform essential services to faculty and students, sufficient technical and clerical help shall be provided.

8.6 *Selection Policy.* The professional staff shall develop a statement of policy, with board approval, for the selection of reference materials, instructional materials for the library, and textbooks.

8.7 *Classroom Instructional Materials and Equipment.* Adequate and appropriate types of teaching and learning materials and equipment for all areas of the school program shall be provided in the amount and type needed to accomplish the instructional objectives.

8.8 *Records.* Records of acquisition, classification, cataloging, circulation, and financing shall be accurate and up to date. An alphabetically arranged card catalog, using a recognized system, and a shelf list shall be maintained.

PROGRESS CRITERIA

—Professional staff hold master's degrees in library science and/or audiovisual and are provided with sufficient technical assistance to adequately perform services.

—A minimum collection of 6,000 books, or 10 books per pupil for larger schools, is provided.

—Independent study spaces (carrels) are provided for a substantial number of students along with rooms for small group discussions.

—Careful study is made of advances in electronic learning devices and appropriate efforts are made to incorporate them for use in the library facility. A modern information retrieval system should be an important objective of the faculty and administration.

—Teachers' offices are in close proximity to the library in order to foster easy communication.

—A faculty advisory committee has been appointed to extend the services and utilization of the library and to evaluate its effectiveness.

Notes

1. *Webster's Third New International Dictionary of the English Language, Unabridged* (Springfield, Mass.: G. & C. Merriam Company, 1965).
2. Adams, Charles W. "The School Media Program: A Position Statement," *School Media Quarterly*, Winter 1974, pp. 127–143.
3. Good, Carter V., ed. *Dictionary of Education*, 3rd ed. (New York: McGraw-Hill, 1973).
4. Harris, Lewis E., and Moore, Clyde B. *Keys to Quality*. Quest for Quality Series. Booklet no. 14. (Washington, D.C.: American Association of School Administrators, 1960), p. 7–8.
5. National Study of Secondary School Evaluation. *Evaluative Criteria*, 4th ed. National Study of Secondary School Evaluation. Distributed by the American Council on Education (Washington, D.C.: American Council on Education, 1969).
6. National Study of Secondary School Evaluation. *Evaluative Criteria for Junior High Schools*, 2nd ed. National Study of Secondary School Evaluation. Distributed by the American Council on Education. (Washington, D.C.: American Council on Education, 1970).

7. American Association of School Librarians; A.L.A.; and Association for Educational Communications and Technology. *Media Programs: District and School* (Chicago: American Library Association, 1975), p. viii.
8. Ellsworth, Ralph E. *The School Library: Facilities for Independent Study in the Secondary School*, by Ralph E. Ellsworth and Hobart D. Wagener, edited by Ruth Weinstock. (New York: Educational Facilities Laboratories, 1963).
9. Henne, Frances. "School Libraries." In *Library Surveys*, edited by Maurice F. Tauber and Irene R. Stephens. (New York: Columbia University Press, 1967).
10. Henne, Frances; Ersted, Ruth; and Lohrer, Alice. *A Planning Guide for the High School Library Program* (Chicago: American Library Association, 1951).
11. Erickson, Carlton W. H. *Administering Instructional Media Programs* (New York: Macmillan, 1968), p. 626.
12. *Ibid.*, p. 627.
13. Kansas State Department of Education. *Bulletin 201: Rules, Regulations, Standards, and Procedures for Accrediting Elementary Schools* Filed Jan. 1, 1975, effective date September 1, 1975. (Topeka: Kansas State Department of Education, 1975), pp. 10–14.
14. Kansas State Department of Education. *Bulletin 101: Rules, Regulations, Standards, and Procedures for Accrediting Junior High Schools.* Filed Jan. 1, 1975, effective Sept. 1, 1975. (Topeka: Kansas State Department of Education, 1975), pp. 14–15.
15. Kansas State Department of Education. *Bulletin 201: Rules, Regulations Standards, and Procedures for Accrediting High School.* Filed Jan. 1, 1975, effective Sept. 1, 1975. (Topeka: Kansas State Department of Education, 1975), pp. 18–22.
16. North Central Association of Colleges and Secondary Schools. *Policies and Standards for the Approval of Junior High/Middle Schools, 1973–1974* (Chicago: North Central Association of Colleges and Secondary Schools, 1974), p. 36–38.
17. North Central Association of Colleges and Secondary Schools. *Policies and Standards for the Approval of Secondary Schools, 1974–1975* (Chicago: North Central Association of Colleges and Secondary Schools, 1975), pp. 31–33.

For Further Reading

Adams, Charles W. "The School Media Program: A Position Statement." *School Media Quarterly,* Winter 1974, pp. 127–143.

American Association of School Librarians. *Standards for School Library Programs.* Chicago: American Library Association, 1960.

American Association of School Librarians, and Association for Educational Communications and Technology. *Media Programs: District and School.* Chicago: American Library Association, Washington, D.C.: and Association for Educational Communications and Technology, 1975.

American Association of School Librarians, and Department of Audiovisual Instruction. *Standards for School Media Programs*. Chicago: American Library Association, and Washington, D.C.: National Education Association, 1969.

Davies, Ruth Ann. *The School Library: A Force for Educational Excellence*. 2nd ed. New York: Bowker, 1974.

DeProspo, Ernest R., and Samuels, Alan R. "A Program Planning and Evaluation Self-Instructional Manual." In *Media Program Evaluation in an Accountability Climate: Proceedings of the AASL Special Program*, San Francisco, June 29, 1975, edited by James W. Liesener. Chicago: American Library Association, 1976).

Ellsworth, Ralph E., and Wagener, Hobart D. *The School Library: Facilities for Independent Study in the Secondary School*. New York: Educational Facilities Laboratory, 1963.

Erickson, Carlton W. H. *Administering Instructional Media Program*. New York: Macmillan, 1968.

Fulton, William R. *Criteria Relating to Educational Media Programs in School Systems*. (Prepared under auspices of the U.S. Office of Education.) Norman, Okla.: University of Oklahoma, 1966.

Gaver, Mary. *Effectiveness of Centralized Library Services in Elementary Schools*. 2nd ed. New Brunswick, N.J.: Rutgers University Press, 1963.

Gaver, Mary. *Patterns of Development in Elementary School Libraries Today: A Five-Year Report on Emerging Media Centers*. 3d ed. Chicago: Encylcopaedia Britannica, 1969.

Gaver, Mary. *Services of Secondary School Media Centers: Evaluation and Development*. Chicago: American Library Association, 1971.

Gaver, Mary V., and Jones, Milbrey L. "Secondary Library Services: A Search for Essentials." *Teachers College Record* 68 (December 1966): 200–210.

Gaver, Mary V., and Scott, Marian. *Evaluating Library Resources for Elementary School Libraries*. New Brunswick, N.J.: Rutgers University Press, 1962.

Gillespie, John T., and Spirt, Diana L. *Creating a School Media Program.* New York: Bowker, 1973.

Gordon, Roger L., ed. "An Evaluative Look at the Standards for School Media Programs." A Report of the 1970 Northeast Regional Audiovisual Leadership Conference, Jan. 22–24, 1970. Philadelphia: Temple University, 1970.

Grazier, Margaret. "Effects of Change on Education for School Librarians." *Library Trends* 17 (April 1969): 410–423.

Henne, Frances. Instruction on the Use of the Library and Library Use by Students." In *Conference on the Use of Printed and Audiovisual Materials for Instructional Purposes,* edited by Maurice F. Tauber and Irene R. Stephens. New York: Columbia University School of Library Service, 1966.

Henne, Frances; Ersted, Ruth; and Lohrer, Alice. *A Planning Guide for the High School Library Program.* Chicago: American Library Association, 1951.

Iowa Department of Public Instruction. *Plan for Progress . . . in the Media Center K-6.* Des Moines: The Department, 1969.

Kansas State Department of Education. *Bulletin 301: Rules, Regulations, Standards, and Procedures for Accrediting Elementary Schools.* Topeka: Kansas State Department of Education, 1975.

Kansas State Department of Education. *Bulletin 101: Rules, Regulations, Standards, and Procedures for Accrediting Junior High Schools.* Topeka: Kansas State Department of Education, 1975.

Kansas State Department of Education. *Bulletin 201: Rules, Regulations, Standards, and Procedures for Accrediting High Schools.* Topeka: Kansas State Department of Education, 1975.

Lane, Margaret. "A Study of School Library Resources in Oregon as Compared to State and National Standards." Ph.D. dissertation. Seattle: University of Washington, 1966.

Liesener, James W. *A Systematic Process for Planning Media Programs.* Chicago: American Library Association, 1976.

Lowrie, Jean Elizabeth. *Elementary School Libraries.* Meutchen, N.J.: Scarecrow Press, 1970.

Lumsdaine, A. A. "Instruments and Media of Instruction." In *Handbook of Research on Teaching*, edited by Nathaniel L. Gage, pp. 582–683. Chicago: Rand McNally, 1963.

Michigan Curriculum Program, assisted by the Michigan Library Association. *Mr. Administrator: What Is Your Library Service Profile?* Lansing: Michigan State Library, 1960.

National Education Association Research Division. "The Secondary-School Teacher and Library Services." Research Monograph M-1, 1958. Washington, D.C.: National Education Association, 1958.

National Study of Secondary School Evaluation. *Evaluative Criteria.* Form F. 4th ed. School Library/Instructional Materials Center. Washington, D.C.: American Council on Education, 1969.

National Study of Secondary School Evaluation. *Evaluative Criteria for Junior High Schools.* 2d ed. National Study of Secondary School Evaluation, distributed by the American Council on Education. Washington, D.C.: American Council on Education, 1970.

New Jersey Department of Education. *Public and School Library Services Bureau. New Jersey Blueprint for School Media Programs.* Trenton, N.J.: The Department, 1970.

New York Library Association. School Libraries Section. *Evaluating the School Library: Suggestions for Studying the School Library in Action.* New York: New York Library Association, 1962.

New York State Educational Communications Association. *New York State Educational Communications Standards.* Albany: New York State Education Department, 1970.

Nickel, Mildred L. *Steps to Service: A Handbook of Procedures for the School Library Media Center.* Chicago: American Library Association, 1975.

Norberg, Kenneth., ed. "The Role of the Media Professional in Education: A Position Paper Prepared for the Board of Directors of the Department of Audiovisual Instruction, National Education Association." *Audiovisual Instruction* 12 (December 1967): 1026–29.

North Carolina State Department of Public Instruction. *Check-*

list for the Library Quarters. Raleigh, N.C.: State Department of Public Instruction, 1963.

North Carolina State Department of Public Instruction. *Developing a Good School Library Program.* Raleigh, N.C.: State Department of Public Instruction, 1961.

North Central Association of Colleges and Secondary Schools. *Policies and Standards for the Approval of Junior High/Middle Schools, 1973–1974.* Chicago: North Central Association of Colleges and Secondary Schools, 1974.

North Central Association of Colleges and Secondary Schools. *Policies and Standards for the Approval of Secondary Schools, 1974–1975.* Chicago: North Central Association of Colleges and Secondary Schools, 1975.

Pennsylvania Department of Public Instruction. *The School Instructional Materials Center and the Curriculum: The Library Audio-Visual Center.* Curriculum Development Series, no. 5. Harrisburg: State Department of Public Instruction, 1962.

Rossoff, Martin. *The Library in High School Teaching.* New York: Wilson, 1955.

Saettler, Paul. "Instructional Technology: Some Concerns and Desiderata." *AV Communication Review* 17 (Winter 1969): 357–67.

Scholl, Joyce B. *Find your School Media Center Service Profile.* Harrisburg: Division of School Libraries. Pennsylvania Department of Public Instruction, 1969.

Southern Association of Colleges and Schools. Committee on Elementary Education. *Evaluating the Elementary School Library Program.* Atlanta: Southern Association of Colleges and Schools, 1964.

Sullivan, Peggy., ed. *Realization: The Final Report of the Knapp School Libraries Project.* Chicago: American Library Association, 1968.

Tiffany, Burton C. "Quality Libraries: A Must for Quality Education." *School Media Quarterly, 4* (Fall 1975): 37–42.

Washington State Superintendent of Public Instruction. *School Library and Audio-Visual Survey.* Olympia, Wash.: State Department of Public Instruction, 1964.

III
Management of Staff
DEVELOPMENT AND TRAINING

There has been little written of decision making in the school library media center, although this process and its results are of vital importance to any library of any size. Theories of management and social psychology outline the implications of participative management or group decision making. Research into the subject shows that group decisions tend to be of quality superior to those that are unilaterally made. In addition, such decisions are more readily accepted by those involved in making them and carrying them out. Involvement of the library staff in decisions and in attaining those objectives arrived at by a participative process will be reflected in the quality of service provided to the users of the library. It is not mandatory or even necessary that this technqiue be used, but staff participation in decision making has been found to be generally characteristic of high production organizations.[1]

The art of library organization and management is probably better in practice than the theory of it as written and presented by leaders in the field. The literature seeks to identify the one best way to organize the library media center in the school. In practice, there are a variety of organizational and managerial styles. The organization and management of the small school library media center will be very different from that of the city

school. The experienced and thoughtful library media specialist recognizes the differences and structures administration
and management accordingly.

Problems cannot be considered by the type of library in
which they occur; environmental setting is critical. In the
school, this may mean the degree of academic emphasis; the
quality of teaching and the expectations of teachers; and the
variety of user needs and interests. Maurice P. Marchant
studied the characteristics of the library's decision-making
process and the impact on staff satisfaction of that process and
found the above to be true.[2]

The media specialist in the school should consider an open
system of organization which implies that there are several subsystems in the library with varying characteristics and needs.
Decision making on a subsystem basis is effective—that is, the
persons working in a particular area recommend and have a
part in decision making for that particular area of the library
organization. One might consider production, maintenance,
adaptive, and managerial subsystems.[3]

Much of the literature in library management centers still on
the bureaucratic organization in which directors have a high
degree of authority and responsibility. However, the publication of the American Library Association, *Personnel Utilization
in Libraries: a Systems Approach,* by Myrl Ricking and Robert E
Booth, approaches the problem of management and administration from a systems approach, in which the definition of
goals comes well before the identification of tasks; tasks derive
from programs, programs develop in response to stated goals;
stated goals come from the assessment of needs. This is an excellent resource for the small and medium-sized library.[4]

Decision making by those most directly involved in the implementation of a decision or otherwise best suited to determine what the decision should be is not to be taken as the ab-
dication of responsibility by the administrative person at the
top. Rather, it is an opening up a free flow and an exchanging
of ideas and information, group evaluation, and discussion,
with all sharing in the responsibility and reward for the accomplishment of good and effective work.

Management, Including Paraprofessionals, Nonprofessionals,
Technicians, Clerks and Volunteers

Management decision making is closely related to staff management. A staff member who is closely involved in decision-
making has a personal interest and a sense of responsibility for
the decision taken and its effect on the administration of the
library media center. This is true whether the staff member is
a professional, an aide, the media technician, or any other
member of the staff. All staff members must work together in
an effective and productive manner; a share in the responsibility for decisions contributes to a pleasant, friendly situation.

Teaching Staff Involvement

The media specialist who directs the library media center
may consider teaching staff involvement as a morale booster.
Moreover, faculty relationships are improved and better feedback is gained from faculty when staff members are involved
in decision making in the media center. As a result of staff involvement, the faculty appears to be more satisfied with the library media center, the selection of its material, the administration and staffing, and the decisions made in regard to
classroom use of the center. In library media centers observed,
carefully planned staff involvement works well and has many
diverse values.

Library Media Center Staff Involvement

Decisions by members of the library media center staff
should be made in the areas where individuals are best suited
to make them and to facilitate the solving of problems. Staff
persons most closely involved in particular situations or areas
of work can often make the most realistic decisions concerning
these areas. Small group interaction, interaction on a one-to-
one basis, should be encouraged among the staff concerning
problems of mutual concern. Solutions that have evolved with

general approval can then be tried out with all the staff being participants in the success or failure of the decision.

Under participative management, cooperation replaces competition. However, the leadership of the media director and other professionals on the staff should not be minimized. The capacity to analyze feedback and to mediate conflicting views are the marks of a strong leader in the library media center, as in all situations in which individuals work together.

With participative management, the media specialist is, in effect, delegating decision making to the personnel responsible for the task. The media specialist, is, thus, freed from considerable involvement in specific procedural details to consider overall planning and cohesion of all the parts of the program. Creative leadership and the long view are the responsibility of the media specialist director and the mark of the successful one.

Organizational Change and the Library Media Center

The environment of the school and its library media center has a decided effect on media staff management. Organizational change must be in harmony with the community and its school. The library media center must be ever flexible as it seeks to meet the needs of the students, faculty, and community. The ability to adapt in terms of program and service must be evident as the staff, including the media specialist as leader, learns and performs according to changing contingencies. Internal factors, as well as external ones, have an influence on organizational change within the library media center.

The organizational structure of the school district determines to some extent what the individual school library media center can do and influences development and function of the library media center and how it is organized.

Evaluation and Participative Management

Commitment to measurement and evaluation of program effectiveness and staff function, as well as achievement of stated objectives is a requirement for the excellent school media program. Continuing performance and product evaluation is welcomed rather than feared by the adequate and efficient staff, which is functioning on a cooperative, participative basis.

Evaluation is integral to professional integrity; common sense, as well as theories in administration, dictates the need for evaluation as a basis for intelligent decision making. Decisions, actions, and programs must be evaluated on an ongoing basis. Evaluative criteria above all things should be developed by the staff as a whole with the media specialist as leader. Failure to involve staff in development of criteria can point the way to serious deficiency or failure of the program. Needs assessment, goal setting, identification of measurable objectives, programs to fulfill the needs and reach the goals—all are necessary and staff should be involved in each step.

An ability to admit error and failure is basic to honest evaluation in the library media center. If weaknesses or errors are evident, the program must change and respond to unmet needs in a positive way. Self-analysis must be a learning process for the staff; reevaluating, reassessing, and reshaping must be a part of any program.

As Peter Drucker, authority on management in industry, states: "Managing service institutions for performance will increasingly be seen as the central managerial challenge of a devloped society, and its greatest managerial need."[5] He further states that service institutions must define their purposes and functions clearly and acquire a sense of mission that overarches individual goals.[6]

Selection of Staff

A survey of tasks to be performed and staffing needs will result in development of an overall set of policies for the media program. Included in these policies will be a listing of characteristics and capabilities which media personnel should have. Such planning procedures and evaluation must be done periodically to document and support changing needs.

Major categories of service for which personnel are needed should include:

Reference services. In this category are supplying answers to specific questions and providing information as well as direction and referral to various sources in response to user need or request. Bibliographies prepared on request are a part of this service as are direction and guidance in the use of reference sources within and outside of the library media center.

Instruction. Reading development and guidance in reading are an important part of this service, as are instructional activities in relation to the library media center and its organization. Viewing of audiovisual materials, formal and informal instruction within the library media center or in the classroom are all a part of this instruction. Independent study is a goal of instruction in the use of media so that the student or user becomes independent and responsible in the use of all media within the library media center.

Use of Materials and Equipment. This broad area of work simply means that personnel must be trained and available to provide convenient access and direction in the use of many collections of both print and nonprint materials and the equipment for their use. Loan arrangements for such materials and equipment must be a part of this service. Ease of access is basic to the total library media center program.

Consultation. This category refers to consultation with teachers and with media center staff. Advice and guidance in the selection of materials, in the use of those materials in the classroom, and in the preplanning of curricula are all a part of the library media center's work with the teaching staff of the school. Instructional planning for the individual student or for the class includes participation in departmental planning as well as with the individual teacher.

Production. The production of new or adapted materials for the teacher in the classroom or for the student doing research are a part of this service category. This may involve the actual production of the materials or may include guidance for the student or teacher who will produce the materials independently.

The media specialist-director must have a hand in selection of staff for the school library media center, as well as in other areas of management. Of the three major components of the school library media program—materials, facilities, and personnel—the most important, the one that melds and provides engine power for the other two, is personnel. In the words of Burton C. Tiffany, recipient of the 1975 Distinguished Library Service Award for School Administrators, Chula Vista, California: "Good people, adequate in number with essential personal and professional competencies are most important."[7]

Categories of Staff: Media Center Tasks Identified

School library media programs must be adequately supported by staff if they are to meet the needs of the school and of the individual learner. Full services of the media program imply many functions and tasks requiring different levels of competency and training. Differentiated staffing, therefore, is implied when the great variety of tasks to be performed in the library media center are recognized. Those positions at the professional level are discussed fully in *Certification Model for Professional Media Personnel*, and there are now statements of competency level for support staff—clerical, technical, and paraprofessional personnel.[8] However, there is a need for the individual library media center to develop position classification with job descriptions. Such job descriptions should state the supportive tasks which will be performed under the direction of the library media specialist, qualifications for various positions, and the relationship with the professional staff.

Library Media Aide. The person who holds the broad-based position as library media aide performs many basic clerical and secretarial tasks. The aide may supervise distribution of audio-visual equipment, use of duplicating and projection equipment, and many additional duties, such as helping to supervise student library assistants. The aide works under the direct supervision of the professional media specialist.

The library media aide must be a responsible, mature, and congenial person who has the ability to follow oral and written directions, carry through with assigned duties, and follow the established procedures, rules, and regulations of the library media center. The aide should work well with both faculty and students and should be at least a high school graduate with clerical and secretarial training. Many college graduates find satisfaction and do an excellent job in media aide positions.

Library Media Technician. In some library media centers, one person may perform the functions of both technician and aide. However, the technician position requires knowledge and skills that are unique to library media center work, such as mechanical knowledge of the audiovisual equipment for repair and maintenance; of computer technology (when applicable); of TWX (teleprinter-to-teleprinter) equipment and its use in library communications; of the circulation system of the library media center; of television and videorecording; of graphics and photography. The library media technician must know established library media center procedures and work effectively within the system.

The training of the media technician may be formal or informal, on-the-job training, or other training which is sufficient to enable him to perform needed specific functions in the library media center. A number of community colleges and technical institutions now offer courses for media technicians, leading to an associate (two-year) degree.

The media technician supports the professional staff by performance of tasks of a specialized nature. He works under the supervision of the media specialist, but must be able to make independent decisions and must know the operation of the library media center.

The media technician may supervise those who assist him as well as the clerks who keep records of equipment for repair and distribution.

He is a reliable, independent worker who needs little supervision. He should work well with both faculty and staff and be willing to participate in workshops and in-service programs in order to keep abreast of the newest and best in technology and library media center procedures.

Training of Aides and Volunteers

These members of the paraprofessional staff, which may include student aides in the library media center, should be trained and training programs in use should be evaluated frequently. Training should utilize new instructional methods and new concepts of service, and "success" in carrying out the program should be discussed with those involved. Visual aids, an up to date handbook of library procedures, and instructional sheets or manual in regard to particular routines are basic and necessary and consultation with library media specialists on a regional or district basis offers help in determining the best training programs for library media support staff.

On-the-Job-Training. An effective training manual and job descriptions are important to a planned training program. Good instructional and resource materials on a professional level should be available to meet needs of paraprofessionals who are interested in further reading and information. On-the-job training is most effective and the new paraprofessional in the library media center finds observing, practicing, and learning under the direction of an experienced staff member, mostly on a one-to-one basis, both challenging and interesting. Method, length, and type of training depend on the ability and experience of the paraprofessional and the amount of concentrated time and effort the trainer is able to dedicate to training. The program, as in all areas of training, should include both written and visual material, case situations, instructions, and examples. Close supervision and situational, on-the-spot instruction from the professional media specialist are most helpful.

In-Service Training. In-service training sessions or a workshop approach on a district or interlibrary level are often the most practical means of instruction for groups of employees with similar job assignments. Duration can be a few hours, a day, or continuing over several weeks or months.

Usually such sessions are conducted as working site sessions with the library media center used as a setting in which the trainee can have "hands-on" experience and apply specific skills. In-service training has these advantages: definite goals are accomplished within the time frame; experience and problems are shared; specialists can reach a large group of employees at one time and skills are practiced in a real situation.

Workshops. These are a form of in-service training but may be offered by a college or university, a larger school system, or on a district or state level. They may include visits to several nearby media centers. When offered outside the system, they require that the student or paraprofessional adapt the skills learned to practices followed by the media center where the individual is employed. Therefore, workshop planning calls for a more general and less specific approach to procedures and to teaching skills.

Work-study Programs. Many school districts offer work-study programs to prepare students for jobs in business and industry. General skills, usually business and clerical skills, may be practiced in the media center. Proper planning and coordination with the skills being learned and with the coordinator of the work-study program are important. Learned skills such as these can be used effectively in the library media center; a work-study program can lead to recruitment of employees for the future.

Posthigh School Programs. The associate degree program of area community colleges and academic programs of certain schools often contain requirements and electives to provide basic and specialized knowledge in the library media field. The media specialist can well be concerned about this training. Courses in the technical skills of processing and cataloging of both print and nonprint materials, in the routines of the library media center, in preparation of audiovisual materials and in operating, maintaining, and using equipment in the school—all can be offered in the posthigh school program. Such basic training plus fieldwork will provide knowledge and training for work in the library field in the community, in the school, or in industry.

Student Library Aides

Student library aides in the school are often enrolled in a course for which they get credit, as are student classroom aides in the modern school organization. However, a high school library aide program without credit can also be successful. Students today show an interest in volunteer service and so quite willingly contribute such service to the school program.

An instruction manual which may be shared with paraprofessional adult staff is basic to student aide instruction. This, with in-service meetings of the students with the media specialist and much on-the-job training, will meet needs of students and provide for a real contribution to the library media program in the school. An independent study approach to assigned sections of the instruction manual appeals to students as they work at their own pace. Written work utilizing the manual's instructions is a good learning aid. Students should know how to analyze a book, know the technical parts of the book, and be familiar with the reference collection of the library media center.

Processing and Other Procedures

In many smaller schools, book processing still takes place in the individual library media center. Students who are library aides can learn to do the processing of books and enjoy and contribute to these procedures. Incoming books are attractive; students like to check an invoice and to arrange books for further processing by the media specialist and/or library aide. The ability and interest of the student determines the extent of the contribution to processing and a wide range of other procedures, such as:

> invoice checking
> embossing ownership with stamp
> author-title book card slips
> opening of a new book
> attaching plastic jackets on cover (when used)
> pasting pockets, date dues
> check-out and circulation procedures
> shelving of books
> straightening of shelves
> filing of magazines
> securing requested magazines for user
> assembling reserved collection
> display areas preparation

In the selection of library aides for the library media center staff, an application form is valuable and recommended. (An example is found at the end of this chapter.) With the application, the student includes a "contract" which outlines his commitment to serve as a student library aide. Student applicants should be good to excellent academically. They should be dependable, mature, and have integrity and a cooperative attitude. Such characteristics may be noted by teachers or other adults who recommend the student library aide.

In the selection of the student library aide, the student's schedule must be considered so that students have the opportunity to enroll in needed and desired academic courses in the school but can still contribute to the library media center on a credit or volunteer basis. The number of students who can serve as student library aides will vary with the size of the library media center. An attitude of respect, of consideration for the needs of other students and faculty, and the climate of an efficiently operating library media center are basic to student library assistance in the center. The student can make an important contribution to the atmosphere of the center as many students coming to the media center enjoy and appreciate being served by another student. It gives students the feeling that the library media center really belongs to them and that they have some degree of responsibility for its operation.

One of the best sources of reference for the library media specialist in regard to paraprofessional support staff is: *Paraprofessional Support Staff for School Media Programs: A Competency Statement*, prepared by the Certification of School Media Specialist Committee, American Association of School Librarians (a division of the American Library Association), published by the American Library Association in 1978.[9]

Certification Standards for School Media Center Staff

The educational preparation of the library media specialist in today's school is essentially different from that of the traditional librarian. The explosion of knowledge and new technologies have created the need for new competencies in our schools.

There is no nationally recognized process for educating and

certifying school media professionals. The media specialist's certification in each state should be compatible with certification requirements and practices for other educational personnel in that state. The design for such certification should be planned, examined, and updated frequently by groups broadly representative of media specialists, of professional organizations, state department of education personnel, and representatives from academic institutions preparing school media professionals.

There should be more than one level of entry for media professionals and such levels should be based on the degree of capability attained within each competency area. Methods of measuring competency vary from state to state. Much study has been done on a state level and by such national organizations as the American Association of School Librarians' School Library Manpower Project, which was carried out in three phases between 1968 and 1974. This work was preceded by the Standards for School Library Programs (A.L.A., 1960); the Knapp School Libraries Demonstration Project (1963–1968); and the National Inventory of Library Needs (A.L.A., 1965). In 1971, a task force of the Association for Educational Communications and Technology was established and held hearings and reviews for a two-year period. The guidelines from this study emphasize the need for competency-based levels of entry and set forth nine basic media functions.[10]

Candidates for professional certification enter the ranks with minimal or basic competencies attained. The certification of such personnel by a state agency is based upon the premise that the candidates for certification have achieved a required level of proficiency. Continued professional development for all personnel within the library media field is an important part of certification standards, regardless of the level of certification entry. The design should provide recognition for the attainment of great degrees of skill within particular areas of competence; lack of this recognition is a weakness in many state certification requirements. Competency requirements should reflect different levels of responsibility, and provide mobility between building- and district-level positions based on competency levels. Methods of measuring competencies will vary but there must be incentives which encourage professionals to strive for higher degrees of capability.

Incentives incorporated within a program of continuing professional education should include:

> Academic courses leading to advanced degrees
> Academic courses or seminars
> In-service programs and workshops
> Workshops or in-service programs on a regional level designed to meet identified needs
> Provision for independent study projects or programs
> Research and further study on specified areas of interest or need
> Practicums available within the region, state, or nation
> Work experiences in a setting different from the school, district, or teaching center
> Planned visitations
> (Note: Such continuing education programs are those provided by The Mountain Plains Library Association.)

Assessment of the Candidate on a Professional Level. There are numerous strategies for assessing candidate qualifications. Such assessments are a part of any evaluation procedure and should involve various groups of persons within the educational community, such as media professionals, other teaching personnel, administrators, professional organization representatives, including the media association, state department of education personnel, and library media educators.

Areas of Competencies. The *Certification Model for Professional School Media Personnel,* developed in 1976 by the Certification of School Media Specialist Committee, American Association of School Librarians, American Library Association, delineates seven major areas of competencies in some detail.[11] These should be studied by any committee developing state certification models or standards. This source is recommended to any media specialist serving as a member of a committee developing certification standards for a state, district, or region. It is the best resource in the field.

INFORMATION FOR STUDENT
LIBRARY MEDIA ASSISTANTS

STUDENT LIBRARY ASSISTANTS:

Student library assistants should be interested in helping students and teachers in the library media center. They should aim to help make the library media center a place conducive to study and relaxation. In order to accomplish these aims, the person working in the library media center should be efficient, knowledgeable about the library media center, and cooperative. He should be quick to learn procedures and should anticipate where he can best serve. His attitude should exemplify sincere interest in patrons and should show that he wants the student or teacher to use the library media center, and to return again.

DUTIES ARE:
1. Work at charge desk
2. Check out materials
3. Take care of passes and ask that students sign the register
4. Shelve materials
5. Help librarian and the aide as requested
   a. Bulletin boards
   b. Checking in magazines and shelving
   c. Operation of the microfilm reader and return of film
   d. Filing of magazines

Generally, the time a student spends in the library should not be considered a study hall. However, one is in school to learn and when one has problems with an assignment, the librarian, if at all possible, will give the student time to study or complete the assignment. Generally, one should not work in the library if he needs time for study.

One-half credit per semester is given for work as a library assistant.

APPLICATION BLANK FOR LIBRARY ASSISTANT

Date _____ 19 _____

NAME _____ Year in school _____

Student assistants are needed in the library to help in extending its services. We continue to have student library assistants as the students themselves find satisfaction in the service they render to their school. The student who works in the library is there because he has elected to be there. The work is meaningful to him as well as to the school. His service to the library is designed to increase its effectiveness without exploiting the student. He will not find duties beyond his capacity or training. He is, however, an invaluable library assistant and an ambassador for his school.

JOB DESCRIPTION

1. Take care of all checking in and checking out of materials.
2. Shelve books and all materials.
3. Shelve current newspapers and periodicals.
4. Assist librarian as directed.

CONTRACT

I understand one-half credit is offered per semester for library assistants.

I understand I will be evaluated against all other applicants when applying for this position.

I understand there will be a three-week probationary period at the end of or during which it will be determined if the work experience is satisfactory to all parties.

I understand there will be two meetings of a directional nature with the librarian. Attendance at these meetings is a part of my grade.

I understand that so long as I can meet the job description requirements, as stated above, I can expect a grade of "P". In order to receive a grade of "P+" I will have to perform and achieve over and above the job description requirements as stated above.

I will do my best to cooperate with librarians, students, and teachers in order that the library can offer the best service to students and teachers. I am interested in seeing that the library is a fitting place for study and relaxation for students and faculty members.

Hour to work _____   _____
                                Signature of applicant

                                _____
                                Librarian

Notes

1. Likert, Rensis. *New Patterns of Management.* (New York: McGraw-Hill, 1961), p. 170.
2. Marchant, Maurice P. "Participative Management as Related to Personnel Development," *Library Trends,* July 1971, pp. 48–59.
3. Katz, Daniel, and Robert L. Kuhn. *The Social Psychology of Organization.* (New York: Wiley, 1966), pp. 39–47.
4. Ricking, Myrl, and Robert E. Booth. *Personnel Utilization in Libraries: A Systems Approach.* (Chicago: American Library Association, 1974).
5. Drucker, Peter. *Management: Tasks, Responsibilities, Practices.* (New York: Harper & Row, 1974), p. 135.
6. Ibid., p. 166.
7. Tiffany, Burton C. "Quality Libraries: A Must for Quality Education," *School Media Quarterly* 4 (Fall 1974): 37–42.
8. Certification of School Media Specialist Committee, American Association of School Librarians. *Certification Model for Professional School Media Personnel.* (Chicago: American Library Association, 1976), pp. 5–7.
9. Certification of School Media Specialist Committee, American Association of School Librarians. *Paraprofessional Support Staff for School Media Programs: A Competency Statement.* (Chicago: American Library Association, 1978).
10. Certification of School Media Specialist Committee, *Certification Model for Professional School Media Personnel.* p. 25.
11. Certification of School Media Specialist Committee. *Certification Model for Professional School Media Personnel.* p. 4.

For Further Reading

Altman, Ellen, and others. *A Data Gathering and Instructional Manual for Performance Measures in Public Libraries.* Chicago: Celadon Press.

Baker, D. Philip. *School and Public Library Media Programs for Children and Young Adults.* Syracuse: Gaylord Professional Publications, 1977.

Certification of School Media Specialist Committee, American Association of School Librarians. *Paraprofessional Support Staff for School Media Programs: A Competency Statement.* Chicago: American Library Association, 1978.

Chisholm, Margaret E., and Ely, Donald P. *Media Personnel in Education: A Competency Approach.* Englewood Cliffs, N.J.: Prentice-Hall, 1976.

Drucker, Peter F. *Management: Tasks, Responsibilities, Practices.* New York: Harper & Row, 1974.

Edwards, G. Edward. *Management Techniques for Librarians.* New York: Academic Press, 1976.

Galvin, Thomas J. "Beyond Survival: Library Management for the Future." *Library Journal* 101 (September 15, 1976): 1833–35.

Gillespie, John T., and Spirt, Diana L. *Creating a School Media Program.* New York: Bowker, 1975.

Govan, James. "The Better Mouse Trap: External Accountability and Staff Participation." *Library Trends* 26 (Fall 1977): 255–67.

Herzberg, Frederick. *Work and the Nature of Man.* Cleveland: World, 1966.

Liesener, James W. *A Systematic Process for Planning Media Programs.* Chicago: American Library Association, 1976.

Likert, Rensis. *The Human Organization: Its Management and Value.* New York: McGraw-Hill, 1967.

Lynch, Beverly P. "The Academic Library and Its Environment." *College and Research Libraries* 35 (March 1974): 126–32.

Marshall, Faye Dix. *Managing the Modern School Library.* West Nyack, N.Y.: Parker Publishing Co., 1976.

Marchant, Maurice. "Participative Management as Related to Personnel Development." *Library Trends,* July 1971, pp. 48–59.

McGregor, Douglas. *The Human Side of Enterprise.* New York: McGraw-Hill, 1950.

Morgan, James E. *Principles of Administrative and Supervisory Management.* Englewood Cliffs, N.J.: Prentice-Hall, 1973.

Pyhrr, Peter A. *Zero-Based Budgeting: A Practical Management Tool for Evaluating Expenses.* New York: Wiley, 1974.

Ricking, Myrl, and Booth, Robert E. *Personnel Utilization in Libraries: A Systems Approach.* Chicago: American Library Association, 1974.

Roethlisberger, F. J. *Management and Morale.* Cambridge: Harvard University Press, 1956.

Stone, Elizabeth W. *Factors Related to the Professional Development of Librarians.* Metuchen, N.J., Scarecrow Press, 1969.

Stueart, Robert D., and Eastlick, John K. *Library Management.* Littleton, Colo.: Libraries Unlimited, 1977.

Sullivan, A. M. *Human Values in Management.* New York: Thomas Crowell, 1968.

Tiffany, Burton C. "Quality Libraries: A Must for Quality Education." *School Media Quarterly,* 4 (Fall 1975): 37–42.

IV
Budgeting and Fiscal Accounting

The aim of this chapter is to present and discuss a view of budgeting and fiscal control for the library media program in order to assist the media specialist in the preparation of the budget. New ideas in budgeting may make the fiscal and budgetary accounting more realistic and workable. The budget is a plan for the future, a chart of the course to be taken. In *Webster's Third New International Dictionary* the word *budget* is defined as a "statement of financial position of a sovereign body for a definite period of time based on detailed estimates of planned and projected expenditures during the period and proposals for financing them . . . a plan for the coordination of resources and expenditures."[1]

The concepts of budgeting according to the Planning, Programming, Budgeting Evaluation System (PPBS) are discussed, as are the Management by Objectives (MBO) concepts. In the media center, it is expected that the budgeting process will outline the program and request required amounts of money to carry it out. Since the budget is a chart for the future, alternative plans must be determined; such plans are considered and decided upon by the media specialist. A budget becomes a statement of policy on which expenditures are based.

Since the media program budget is only a fraction of the total budget of the school district, it is sometimes overlooked or is not increased to keep pace with the demands of the instructional program. It is the responsibility of the media specialist to prepare and present a thorough, well-prepared, comprehensive, and persuasive budget. It must be supported by adequate data. It must strike just the right balance between ambition for the program and careful consideration of fiscal constraints. It is a quantitative statement of philosophy of the library media center and of the media specialist who directs the center and plans the program. It is an expression of the priorities and goals of the media center, the school, and the community. Ideally, it should provide some phasing of desired projects and activities, some alternatives, and some areas of leeway where an acceptable compromise is possible.

Systematic planning of media programs involves many kinds of data, both data previously collected and newly collected. Specific cost data is basic and necessary—the cost of basic resources and the cost of using these resources in delivery of information service. Cost accounting, as determined by Mary E. Crankston in one of the earliest attempts to determine costs, is "concerned with the determining of costs of one activity or one unit of work."[2] It should be said, however, that when a new media center is established, it is most important to provide a base for building an initial collection that is a basic collection. This chapter is primarily concerned with the costs of ongoing programs in the media center, not the initial costs of establishing the media center. There must then be continuing systematic investment to develop and maintain up to date and quality collections in the library media center. Professional guidelines provide guidance and direction for the school administrator, of whatever size school, as well as for the media specialist, as they set about determining appropriate budgetary allocations for the library media center.[3] In times of escalating cost of media collections and equipment, it is most important that planning be adequate and careful. Funds which are adequate for today may not provide for purchases in the year or so ahead. There must be that financial consideration. The cost of maintaining a quality program grows as the cost of needed materials, equipment, and necessary technical processes climb. A functional media program which is to support a quality educational program must include up to date materials as well as adequate staff time.

Operating costs are *direct costs* while *indirect costs* include overhead and capital costs. Equipment, in most library media centers, is added to the initial collection from the annual budgetary funds and is considered an operating cost. Supplies are an operating cost. *Direct costs* will include materials of all kinds: equipment, supplies, and staff time (labor). *Indirect costs* include both overhead (to include administrative services of the school or district), utilities, district media support services (if available), depreciation, and maintenance. Capital expenditures are considered an indirect cost, such as physical facilities, initial equipment, and original purchase of such items. The production of materials and supplies is considered in some budgeting procedures to be overhead. They can and do contribute to service outputs.

Unfilled Requests from User

As the media specialist sets up the budgetary presentation, it is recommended that an item "unfilled requests from user" be included. This will facilitate the provision of those needed materials or equipment, or even staff time. An unfilled request is one request for a specific service that the media staff cannot provide. Reasons may be lack of space, lack of staff, or similar reasons.

Report of Holdings

The current holdings report (number of items in collection at present), the number of items added, and the number replaced should be a part of the records for the year and of the annual report of the library media center. It may not be used for cost calculations but is valid information. Methods of counting items must be consistent and defined in the report.

Staff Time and Services

A similar report of staff time and services is recommended to include services identified, operational tasks with daily averages of time used to accomplish them. A record of a sample of days of staff time utilization should be kept to support the staff time and services accounting procedure. These sample days should be representative of the year. A staff member is asked to keep a diary or a time log for a specific number of days.

Sources of Financial Support

Money for education comes from the state and national governments, as well as from local taxes. The media specialist must be well informed about the programs of the federal government in the library media area. Such information usually comes from the state department of education or from library media consultants for the state. There are frequent changes in educational funding. Since 1958, when the first law providing funds to elementary and secondary education became operational, the federal government has provided supplementary educational monies available for media programs through the various titles of NDEA (National Defense and Education Act) and ESEA (Elementary and Secondary Education Act). In fiscal 1980 there were 171 millions of dollars allocated for school library and media resources in the schools. These funds are allocated through the states and local school districts on a per capita formula basis. A few states provide some funds for school library media program support: North Carolina allocates $8.00 per capita for instructional materials and supplies; Tennessee $2.00 per capita; and Wisconsin and Louisiana $1.23 and $1.00 respectively. In Hawaii, all schools are state funded and the amount allocated to library purposes is determined by individual school principals. The U.S. Office of Education and the National Institute of Education (NIE) occasionally have made funds available and directed special programs for the schools. The Right-to-Read program undertaken by the USOE is illustrative of the selective and innovative character of these grants and programs. The National Endowment for the Arts and Humanities has made some funding available to schools that can impact on the library program—poets or "artists" in the schools, for example.

The school media specialist must be imaginative about tapping into funds for education that are *not* labeled "library" "media" or "resources." Recent examples are public laws which provide large amounts of federal money for "mainstreaming" handicapped children into the schools. He must be alert to opportunities to request that funds for supporting materials are included in grant proposals for all curricular areas.

Regional and special local funds are sometimes available. In California, for example, school libraries rely on unified and county support for audiovisual materials. Contractual agreements, such as those for instructional television, are in effect in many areas of the country. Local funds may sometimes be available for special purposes by making specific proposals to organizations or businesses. Special grants sometimes come from professional organizations, such as the American Library Association for demonstration or model purposes.

Goals and Objectives

With the emphasis on program budgeting, long-range goals for the media center must be established. National, state, and regional standards and guidelines include basic material for shaping local goals. School officials and administrators are often influenced in their decisions about school media programs and funding by such standards and they should be briefly summarized in their rationale of the budget plan. An area survey, a survey of school districts of like size, or a summary survey of the national or state professional library or educational communications and technology organization is basic to the budgetary proposal, as well.

The concept of management by objectives, or program budgeting, makes its budget demands quite clear. It means, simply, that instead of allocating to the library media center a given sum based on some externally arrived at and often irrelevant rule of thumb, the budget allocation relates directly to the program and activities that have been projected. It links resources inextricably to management and performance.

Existing Collections

The media specialist must develop and present a comprehensive picture of the media center's collection, which includes all existing holdings in books, in audiovisual media, equipment, and services considered in the light of specific instructional needs and all of the standards in the field. A *Materials Inventory* is useful; a *Checklist* will compare the holdings of the school library media center with recommendations in terms of numbers (of books, film strips, etc.), as well as specific titles recommended by authoritative professional sources. This checklist can be used as an orderly plan for adding to the collection in order to bring the holding of the library media center up to quality level. The same process can be used for equipment, using an

Equipment Inventory Checklist

Data gathering instruments which are recommended include: *Part I: Physical Resources and Services Data* and *Part II: Staff Time and Services Data of the School Library Media Program Data Collection Guide No. 2.* These are available from Student Supply Store, University of Maryland, College Park, MD 20742. The author is James W. Liesener, a leader in the systematic assessment of media programs and in the development of sophisticated management tools for improving the capability of media specialists to articulate and develop more responsive and effective programs.

The media specialist then must be always on the lookout for materials to update and meet needs as they arise. In preparing a budget the cost of materials in relationship to educational need makes good sense to the administrator, to the board of education, and to the community. It can be seen by them; it shows what the money can buy and what is needed. A graphic presentation or chart is most effective. An itemized budget is mandatory; it is effective and convincing. Performance budgeting, Management by Objectives, cost-effectiveness analysis, and Planning-Programming-Budgeting (PPBS) are systems to consider in budgeting for the library media center program.

Performance Budgeting

Activities budgeting or functional budgeting are synonymous with performance budgeting. Such budgeting is stated in terms of work to be done or activities to be carried out, with compiled cost standards and work measurements applied to each activity. Thus, a dollar total for each activity is arrived at. It is management oriented and seeks to obtain the maximum amount of activity at the lowest unit cost. The budget document stresses identification of activities and their units.

Management by Objectives

This is a broad term used, in effect, to describe PPBS—Planning, Programming, Budgeting System. The literature shows agreement in that such systems of management include (1) system concept and output orientation; (2) identifiable and measurable outputs; (3) stated objectives; (4) consideration of alternative means to achieve objectives; (5) activities grouped into program categories; (6) measured progress toward objectives; (7) analysis of benefits in relation to costs; and (8) long-range planning.

Object of Expenditures

Line-item budgets or object of expenditure budgets describe the most common type of budgeting in American government. Such budgets include all of the items and services for which expenditures are made. They are easy to prepare and to understand, and accountability is the main advantage of object of expenditure budgets. Disadvantages include the fact that the ease of preparation and the budget process tend to project past policy decisions into the future budget with all budget items growing without concern for objectives of the program. This budget process cannot provide accountability for the performance or accomplishment of an objective; it is very effective in increasing accountability for dollars and cents.

Cost-effectiveness Analysis

Useful cost-effective analysis compares alternatives in terms of differences in effectiveness for the same costs (the comparison of outputs). In other words, it compares differences in costs for the same effectiveness, the comparison of inputs for an identical output.

PPBS

The technique of PPBS—Planning, Programming, Budgeting System—is one of systems analysis with specification of goals, a demonstration of utilization of manpower, resources and facilities, a delineation of priorities among multiple alternatives, and evaluation of output.

PPBS is the newest system of budgeting and is a complex and detailed result of the performance budgeting concept. It is an emphasis on changes in people rather than on materials and costs to bring about changes. It is of value to the school district as it focuses on community attention to support for programs rather than on money spent for facilities or resources.

> planning—to determine and project educational and instructional objectives and the criteria to evaluate the results of such programs under PPBS, at least for five years with projected costs and anticipated results.
> programming—activities, alternative means of achieving the objectives of the project planning. PPBS starts each year at *zero* financial base, sometimes using last year's budget as a model for the current year. Objectives are examined in terms of the year's results, ap-

plying the criteria established in the planning stage.
Objectives may be changed; alternatives established.
The system facilitates change and guards against a
no-care attitude on the part of teachers and the
community.

budgeting—the recording of both the planning and programming information in both fiscal and program-
budget form. The Department of Defense originated
PPBS and has had success with the system; it is a difficult system for schools to adapt but in some form
is being used by many school districts. Dade County,
Florida, has done a pilot project for the Association
of School Business Officials to develop a PPBS
model which could be used in other school districts.
Electronic calculating will contribute to its use because of the rapid manipulation of coded accounts.

Lump-sum System

Once widely used and presently still in use in many school
districts. Under this system the media specialist has a "lump-
sum amount" for use in the media center. This is not an accurate or good system as it is in no way a "program-budgeting"
approach to the library media center and its considerable contribution to the educational program of the school. It is a system which might be used for an initial amount when establishing the media center collection. From that point on, program
and performance should be considered.

Line-item Budget

Included here although discussed earlier in object of expenditure budgeting. This is an early type budget and is simply a listing of items or services with amounts spent. It is similar to a personal checking account, but is not flexible nor does
it take a program into consideration. Neither lump-sum nor

line-item systems provide for program accountability. Line-item budgeting is rarely used today.

A program budget can be a basis for modern management information systems. Such a program budget groups expenditures by program rather than by accounting category and it requires development and statement of long-term objectives. It does provide management information not available in other budgetary systems. Communication is best under the PPBS system as it requires a quantitative approach to libraries and service. The media specialist must communicate to show exactly how much can be done with an amount of money or the money will go elsewhere. There must be relevance.

In the 1968 Guidelines for Development of Planning-Programming-Budgeting Systems, the Bureau of the Budget required four major parts for program budgets:[4]

1. Program Structure. An objective-oriented classification of all activities, broken down into program categories with subcategories and program elements.

2. Program Memoranda (PM's). A statement of the program issues with comparison of cost and effectiveness of alternatives for resolving those issues in relation to objectives with reasons for decisions. They are the documentation for strategic decisions recommended for the budget year.

3. Special Analytic Studies (SAS's). These are the analytic groundwork for decisions reflected in the PM's.

4. Program and Financial Plans (PFP's). A comprehensive multiyear summary of programs in terms of output, cost, and financing needs over a planning period covering the budget year and at least four future years.

PERT

Program Evaluation and Review Technique is a statistical technique for management planning, programming, control of resources, time, and technology in order to achieve program objectives. PERT is a probabilistic technique which may be used to estimate continuously the probability of program completion.

Guiding principles for budgeting are given in the new *Media Programs: District and School,* published by ALA and AECT in 1975.[5] The standards state:

> "To maintain an up-to-date collection of materials and equipment that fulfills and implements the instructional program, the annual per student expenditure of a school district should be at least 10 percent of the national Per Pupil Operational Cost (PPOC), as computed by the United States Office of Education. According to the OSOE definition, the PPOC includes the cost of administration, instruction, attendance services, health services, pupil transportation services, operation of the plant, maintenance of plant and fixed charges, computed on an average daily attendance."

Basic to the budget presentation to the board of education and the superintendent of the district is the cooperation of the faculty, school administrator, and library media specialist, working together to develop a budget request and presentation which adequately represents and presents a monetary plan for what the school is teaching and for the way the media center is used. Knowledge of state, local, and federal support must be incorporated into that presentation of budget. The proposal should be approved by the media coordinator, the school administrator, and the media specialist in the school, who, no doubt, has done most of the work in preparation, although cooperatively. As the media specialist meets with the board of education, or previous to that meeting in discussion with the administrators, items to be discussed and considered together must include:

> *order authority*—the process to be followed in placing orders with the business office, who makes the final decision on orders, determines if they must be presented to the administrator for approval, etc.
>
> *fund encumbering and accounting*—the media specialist must

understand the system of accounting as used by the
school district and set up books and records to
correspond.

small funds ordering—procedures and an amount of money
available in the activities fund are important to the
media specialist to provide for small items needed at
once, or items too small to be processed through the
business office; records for this must be maintained,
as well.

end-of-year reporting—an annual report of acquisitions,
money spent or money on hand must be prepared;
this is used in the budget preparation and is a necessary record; this will include any monies spent
over or under budgeted amounts.

Summary

Since the advent of program budgeting, school media specialists are involved in budgeting, where formerly the distance
was great between the media manager and the administrative
levels. Today the library media specialist must know how much
it costs to operate a media program and must welcome the opportunity to be a part of the budgeting process. Such participation gives the media specialist an opportunity to talk about
media services, what is going on, and what needs to be done,
this year and next, and what it is going to cost and where
monies have gone and for what. This is important as one considers budgeting in a planning-programming-budget system.
By whatever name or method, such planned programs and
budgets do not just happen. A comprehensive management
system must be devised to fit the needs, the system, the school
district, and its administrator.

In many cases, the program structure and description, the
financial plan and evaluation structure are developed at the
same time as the new system is operating. It has been and is
time consuming. Expenditures are, even in the small school
system, more than most media specialists beginning the analy-

zation realize—it is a large budget if all costs are assigned to the program.

It is recommended that the school district which uses the traditional line-item budget format also coordinate a program budget, based on management by objectives in order to dually present this with the line-item budget for discussion and approval. It will show to administrators and board the uses to which materials and equipment are put. A program budget or a management by objectives (MBO) presentation will make costs visible. In other words, money to be spent in the media center will be specifically detailed, to support teaching in the classroom and to meet student individual needs. This should include all media center needs, such as materials, equipment, supplies, maintenance, contractual purchases, personnel, if paid from the media center budget. Whether we are considering program budgeting or management-by-objectives budgeting, we must consider costs in relation to results in relation to goals; we must make costs visible. Our assessment should be of results, not efforts—nor of money spent.

Suggestions for the Library Media Specialist in the School

This chapter has summarized the varying approaches to budgeting in the library media center. The media specialist has an unlimited opportunity to develop a budget which is up to date and which is based on program and services in the center. It is most important that a careful review of budgeting policies be made as they are in the school district and that a budget be developed which correlates with the district budgeting and accounting policies. The For Further Reading section of this chapter gives additional information which may prove useful. A coordinated program budget based on management-by-objectives concepts should be developed in schools where a line-item budget must also be used. It is necessary to be able to show to administrators, to board of education members, and to the community that money is carefully and wisely spent. It is most important that a quality program in the library media

QUANTITATIVE STANDARDS/MATERIALS INVENTORY CHECKLIST

Item	1975 Standards	Present Collection	State Standards
Books			
Paperbacks			
Filmstrips			
Maps			
Charts			
Motion pictures			
16 mm			
8 mm			
8 mm super			
Pamphlets			
Periodicals			
Newspapers			
Microfilm			
Books			
Periodicals			
Newspapers			
Slides			
Recordings			
Disc			
Tape			
Cassette			
Videotapes			
EVR			
Flat pictures			
Transparencies			
Kits			
Programmed materials			
Sound filmstrips			

center be supported by a carefully planned and presented media budget, which is visible, accurate, and well-considered.

Budgeting must be a political process—it is within the framework of the educational unit; it is developed with people and program; it involves the whole staff. The media specialist must be persuasive as he presents the media program and its goals and needs. He must create in the community a climate favorable to the support of these media services. The media program budget is the financial statement of its activities and program. There must be program structure, program memoranda, a financial plan, and an evaluation statement.

In the section, "School Collections," in the latest standards *Media Programs: District and School,* it is stated, "It is recommended that a school with 500 or fewer students have a minimum collection of 20,000 items or 40 per student. The statement continues. "It is possible that the collection in larger schools may provide the needed range in content, levels, forms of expression, and formats at a ratio of less than 40 items per student."[6]

A dollar amount needed for the media center collection is not stated in the new standards. However, many states still have, and believe they need a statement of size and amount of money to maintain a collection adequate for the educational program of the school. (See chapter on Evaluation of the Program of the Library Media Center.)

Notes

1. *Webster's Third New International Dictionary of the English Language, Unabridged* (Springfield, Mass.: G. & C. Merriam Company, 1965).
2. Mary E. Crankston. *Unit Costs in a Selected Group of High School Libraries* U.S. Office of Education Bulletin no. 11 (Washington, D.C.: U.S. Government Printing Office, 1941), p. 5.
3. American Library Association, and Association for Educational Communications and Technology. *Media Programs: District and School.* (Chicago: American Library Association, 1975).
4. U.S. Executive Office of the President, Bureau of the Budget. *Bulletin no. 68–9* (Washington, D.C.: U.S. Government Printing Office, 1968).

5. American Library Association/Association for Educational Communications and Technology. *Media Programs: District and School* (Chicago: American Library Association, 1975), pp. 40–41.

For Further Reading

American Library Association, and Association for Educational Communications and Technology. *Media Programs: District and School.* Chicago: American Library Association, 1975.

Bromberg, Erik. "Simplified PPBS for the Librarian." Prepared for a pre-Conference Institute sponsored by the Library Administration Division of the American Library Association at Dallas, Texas, June 17–19, 1971.

Brown, James W., and Norberg, Kenneth. *Administering Educational Media.* New York: McGraw-Hill, 1972.

Crankston, Mary E. *Unit Costs in a Selected Group of High School Libraries.* U.S. Office of Education Bulletin no. 11. Washington, D.C.: U.S. Government Printing Office, 1971.

Daniel, Evelyn H. "Performance Measurement for School Libraries." In *Advances in Librarianship,* edited by Melvin J. Voight, and Michael H. Harris. New York: Academic Press, 1976.

Davies, Ruth Ann. *The School Library: A Force for Educational Excellence.* New York: Bowker, 1974.

DeProspo, Ernest R., and Liesener, James W. "Media Program Evaluation: A Working Framework." *School Media Quarterly* 3 (Summer 1975): 289–301.

Dorsey, John W. "Planning-Programming-Budgeting (PPB)." *NEA Research Bulletin,* October 1969, pp. 94–95.

Dougherty, R. M., and Heinritz, Fred J. *Scientific Management of Library Operations.* Metuchen, N.J.: Scarecrow Press, 1966.

Erickson, Carlton W. H. *Administering Instructional Media Programs.* New York: Macmillan, 1968.

Gaver, Mary V. *Services of Secondary Media Centers: Evaluation and Development.* Chicago: American Library Association, 1971.

Gillespie, John T., and Spirt, Diana L. *Creating a School Media Program*. New York: Bowker, 1973.

Hanna, Mary Ann. "Instructional Media Centers." *The Michigan Librarian*, Winter 1970, pp. 4–5.

Hannigan, Jane. "PPBS and School Media Programs." In *Budgeting for Accountability in Libraries: A Selection of Readings*, edited by Gerald R. Shields, and J. Gordon Burke. Metuchen, N.J.: Scarecrow Press, 1974.

Heinritz, Fred J. "Quantitative Management in Libraries." *College and Research Libraries* 31 (July 1970): 232–38.

Horton, Roger L., and Bishop, Kent W. "Keeping Up with the Budget Crunch." *Audiovisual Instruction*, December 1970, pp. 49–51.

Jones, William G. "A Time-Series Sample Approach for Measuring Use in a Small Library." *Special Libraries* 64 (July 1973): 280–84.

Kraft, Donald H., and Liesener, James W. "An Application of a Cost-Benefit Approach to Program Planning: School Media Programs." In *Proceedings of the American Society for Information Science* 10:116–117. American Society for Information Science, 1973.

Lancaster, F. W. *The Measurement and Evaluation of Library Services*. Washington, D.C.: Information Resources Press, 1977.

Liesener, James W. "A Planning Process for School Library/ Media Programs." In *Issues in Media Management*, edited by David R. Bender, p. 31–44. Maryland State Department of Education, Division of Library Development and Services, 1973.

Liesener, James W. *A Systematic Process for Planning Media Programs*. Chicago: American Library Association, 1976.

Liesener, James W., and Evitan, Karen M. *A Process for Planning School Media Programs: Defining Service Outputs, Determining Resource and Operational Requirements, and Estimating Costs*. College of Library and Information Services, University of Maryland, 1972.

McCauley, Elfrieda "Budgeting for School Media Service." *School Media Quarterly*, Winter 1976, pp. 126–134.

Nickel, Mildred L. *Steps to Service: A Handbook of Procedures for*

the School Library Media Center. Chicago: American Library
Association, 1975.

Sellers, David Y. "Basic Planning and Budgeting Concepts for
Special Libraries." *Special Libraries* 64 (February 2, 1973).

Shields, Gerald R., and Burke, J. Gordon. *Budgeting for Accountability in Libraries: A Section of Readings.* Metuchen,
N.J.: Scarecrow Press, 1974.

Summers, William. "A Change in Budgetary Thinking," *American Libraries,* December, 1971 pp. 1174–1180.

V

Selection of Materials
in the Library Media Center
in the School

Selection in the library media center of today is an increasingly important function. The *Selection Division* is "the section of an acquisition department or an order department that handles the selection of books." (As defined in the A.L.A. *Glossary of Library Terms with a Selection of Terms in Related Fields*).[1] The resources of the library media center play an ever more basic part in the educational program of the school. The media specialist, in order to select or to coordinate selection wisely, must know the community, the students and their interests, the curriculum of the school as well as the ways in which teachers teach. This means knowing the faculty, knowing their special interests, being receptive to suggestions, and actively seeking them out. A file of suggestions, recommendations, and unfilled wants for book and nonbook materials should be maintained.

There are many variables which influence the information needs of the school, among them: student reading and language skills; the ways in which subjects are taught in the school; trends in teaching; and teacher bias toward subjects which are taught. The alert media specialist who is to fulfill the expanding role that goes with the rising expectations of the library media program must be imaginative, creative, curious, diligent, a person with broad cultural/educational background, impartial, a person of good judgment and good taste, and, above all, a person whose interest in the young person in the school is most evident.

Media selection is an ongoing process, not just a yearly or biyearly procedure. Balancing the benefits of one purchase against another is an unending task. Selection is a part of every request for materials, a part of every conversation in the teachers' lounge; it is basic to the availability or absence of any reference source a student or teacher needs. The daily news, the changing interests of students in areas of the world, a student custom or fad, a new periodical in the library media center, a new review medium in some area of selection—all of these are part of the selection process. Each media center is different and has unique responsibilities in serving the needs of the students and the school.

Materials selected, whether used in the media center, in the classroom, or in the student's home, must have a significant potential in terms of learning or pure recreational enjoyment. No preselected group of materials can adequately serve needs of a particular school, its students, and its teachers. The professional media specialist knows the collection, concentrates on building areas which are weak, adding updated materials where needed. A knowledge of authoritative selection aids and sources which are prepared in the various subject fields as well as in the library media field is valuable. It is helpful, whenever possible, to see the materials at first hand, but a wide collection of review media, bibliographies, and lists will assist greatly in good selection, whether done by the media specialist, by teachers in the classroom, or by student choice. Reporting of local evaluations can be provided for by an acceptable easy-to-use form. (See *New Materials Evaluation Form..*) Workshops on media evaluation are often a part of the program of area selection centers, sponsored by school districts or by library media associations on the state or district level. A complete and up to date section at the end of the chapter lists useful and valuable selection aids. (See *Selection Aids for The Media Specialist, Bibliography of Selection Sources*)

Selection must be systematically organized and should involve all who use materials in the media center or professional library. The *users* of the media center's resources are always the deciding and primary factor in determining additions to the collection.

A good way to involve faculty members in selection is to have an enticing assortment of aids available in the professional library, where they are easily accessible. New materials for preview should be routed to teachers for possible selection. A form for order requests is most useful. (See *Form for Order Requests,* at the end of this chapter.) Students, too, should be involved in selection whenever possible. It is useful evaluative experience for them. Criteria for selection of material should be formulated and used by all. Several *Checklists* are included in this chapter. A checklist alerts a faculty member or student to considerations in making selections. Most important, the goals and the immediate objectives of the library media program, as well as overall selection policy and the criteria for evaluating material and equipment, must be kept before all those who take part in the selection process.

The following activities have worked well in many schools:

1. Involve all areas of the teaching faculty as committees or by informal means in previewing of materials.
2. Maintain a file of reviews and review sources which a teacher may use to find support in selection or aid in evaluation. This may be a collection of selection aids which are available in the professional library or professional collection, supplemented by monthly issues of review periodicals. (See *Selection Aids for the Media Specialist*)
3. Organize and plan for faculty members to visit selection centers in the area or region. Nothing compares to spending a day looking over new materials or equipment.
4. Maintain a file of commercial catalogs for all kinds of media, making them available in the professional library or professional collection.
5. Periodically, provide an exhibit of books and educational materials, on loan as a traveling exhibit or assembled through the cooperation of publishers or vendors.
6. Provide liaison service between the faculty and commercial manufacturers or publishers to obtain whenever needed examination copies, on-loan demonstrations of equipment and on-approval ordering.

7. Ask for purchase selections, utilizing a form for such requests. A busy teacher may have many more suggestions than the one who has more time available. Route selection reviews and bibliographies to them.
8. Conduct workshops and orientation sessions on materials —how to judge their quality and usefulness and how to use them.

Media Selection Policy

A media selection policy is necessary as a part of every center's goals and program. It is basic to all selection procedures. A selection policy is part of the program as recommended by national standards (*Media Programs: District and School,* 1975)[2] and should be cooperatively developed by the staff, consultants, teachers, students, and community representatives under the direction of the district media program and head of the school media program. Such a policy is mandatory for the media program which is to contribute as it should to the educational program. The selection policy is a guideline for the development of the collection; it paves the way for long-range planning to determine program and services. Most important, it protects the teaching integrity of the faculty, the intellectual freedom of the community, and the need of school administrators to do their job without harassment. It can help solve the problem of many schools in regard to controversial materials. The policy provides criteria, identifies selection processes, and makes clear to the community the means by which the collection of the media center is developed. A policy helps with relationships with personnel in the school by making clear the goals and means of accomplishment of those goals in the library media center.

In addition to an approved selection policy, the school library media center should have guidelines to follow for acquisition and selection of all materials and equipment, guidelines which are detailed and specific for the maintenance and building of the collection in all areas.

A selection policy is a statement of:

a school's philosophy
the philosophy of the media center service and program
the goals and objectives of the library media center
a discussion of the means of selection with the persons in-
      volved in selection
a statement of final responsibility and types of materials
      in the collection
a listing of selection aids used
procedures, forms, and ways in which an individual may
      be involved in selection
criteria of selection
procedures for handling complaints with forms used to
      evaluate; forms to reevaluate when so requested

Educational media today is a fast-changing field. New methods of teaching and learning are emerging; effective ways to
teach and learn must be at hand for the classroom teacher and
student to use. The specialist must have opportunities, must
make the opportunity, to see new equipment demonstrated, to
see new media, and to visit centers where the concept of total
media program and service is effectively demonstrated. He
must know new ways to use older media effectively, as well.
Media examination and selection centers and demonstration library media centers should be a part of the program in every
state. There are many excellent sites in the nation, a few in
almost every region; the Knapp School Library Project led the
way for many of the effective demonstration centers.

The budget and the existing collection, as well as perceived
needs and recommendations, are important determining factors in decisions regarding additions to the media collection in
the center and school. The evaluation of the present collection
must be objective, detailed, and supported by facts and figures,
and not a hurried judgment. Criteria for evaluation of the resource collection are available, the best and most up-to-date of
which are included in *Media Programs: District and School*,[3] and
can easily be applied to the existing library media center and
program for comparison.

Selection in the individual school is dependent upon the
services provided by the district or regional center. For exam-

CHECKLIST 1

Book Selection Guide

Author _____ Title _____

Publisher _____ Date _____

Fiction _____ Nonfiction _____ Reference _____ Level _____

Evaluator _____ Recommendation _____

(Evaluation: E-Excellent G-Good F-Fair P-Poor)

Physical Features   E G F P   Comments

Size _____

Binding _____

Paper _____

Print _____

Illustrations _____

Margins _____

Content

Style _____

Literary Quality _____

Organization _____

Presentation _____

Scope _____

Student appeal _____

Special Features

Table of Contents _____

Index _____

Glossary _____

Maps, Diagrams, Charts _____

Potential Use

Specific curriculum _____

Specific reader interest _____

Unique contribution _____

CHECKLIST 2

CRITERIA FOR SELECTING MEDIA AND EQUIPMENT

Authority. Is the material produced by responsible and qualified persons?
Is the equipment produced by reputable manufacturers?

Scope. Is the overall coverage and range of information valid?
How does the material compare to other material in the same subject area?
Does the material have a fresh and challenging viewpoint?

Technical Quality. Is the physical makeup of the material of high quality?
Does it meet acceptable standards?

Format. Would you consider the format used for the transmission of the information a good one, of interest to students and timely?

Authenticity. Is it reliable and valid? Would you consider it as complete a coverage of the information as is possible?
Is it a current copyright date?
Is it timely?

Treatment and arrangement. Is it well organized?
Is the material logically organized?
Is it well balanced as to emphasis?
Would you consider the general comprehension level for students good?
Does it follow sound educational principles?

Aesthetic considerations.
Comment:

Price.

General Considerations. Does the material add to existing collections?
Is it appropriate?
Do you consider that it will be useful?

NEW MATERIALS EVALUATION FORM

To Be Filled Out as New Materials are Previewed Before Purchase

1. Circle: Film Filmstrip Sound Filmstrip Slides Recording
Disc Tape Transparency Chart Graph Map Other

2. Check: _____ Sound _____ Color _____ Black and White
_____ Length

3. Title _____

4. Source or Company _____

5. Producer _____ _____ Copyright date _____

6. Preview date _____ Grade level _____

7. Subject area _____

8. Evaluation _____

Check items which apply to the material
Excellent   Good   Fair   Poor

    a. Teacher's guide; captions; narrative _____

    b. Continuity of outline and content _____

    c. Vocabulary _____

    d. Authenticity of content _____

    e. Quality of:

                Sound _____

                Color _____

                Photography or art work _____

    f. Total instructive value _____

Remarks:

Previewer's signature _____

(Courtesy of Senior High Library Media Center, Wellington, Kansas)

```
ORDER REQUEST FOR THE LIBRARY MEDIA CENTER

TYPE OF MATERIAL _____ (as filmstrip, book, record, etc.)
PERSON MAKING REQUEST _____ DEPARTMENT _____

1. (Title)                              (Author)
   _____

   (Publisher)      (Place of Publication)      Date
   _____

   _____
                                          Price if known
                                          _____

2. (Title)                              (Author)
   _____

   (Publisher)      (Place of Publication)      Date
   _____
                                          Price if known
   _____
                                          _____

3. (Title)                              (Author)
   _____

   (Publisher)      (Place of Publication)      Date
   _____
                                          Price if known
   _____
                                          _____

4. (Title)                              (Author)
   _____

   (Publisher)      (Place of Publication)      Date
   _____
                                          Price if known
   _____
                                          _____
```

ple, expensive films and some equipment can be owned co-operatively and shared. Where there is a lack of centralized resources or services, the school media center must be prepared to take on the tasks of selection, acquisition, and processing in whatever manner meets the needs best. Patterns of organization differ; none is exactly like any other.

A cooperatively developed catalog of all audiovisual material and equipment in the community or the immediate area may include sharing among several types of library media programs and not just among the schools of the district alone.

Media Programs: District and School recommends a base collection for the media program in the school of 20,000 items, inclusive of all types of media, for a school of 500 students. This same ratio is to be adapted to schools of other sizes.

Basic sources to consider in development of a selection policy are:

> *Advisory Statement Concerning Restricted Circulation of Library Materials.* Approved by the Intellectual Freedom Committee, June 20, 1971, as an interpretation of the Library Bill of Rights.
>
> *Advisory Statement on Reevaluating Library Collections.* Adopted by the Intellectual Freedom Committee, June 28, 1972.
>
> *Advisory Statement on Sexism, Racism, and Other "isms" in Library Materials.* Adopted by the Intellectual Freedom Committee, June 25, 1972.
>
> *Freedom on Inquiry, Supporting the Library Bill of Rights:* Proceedings of the Conference on Intellectual Freedom, Jan. 23-24, 1965, Washington, D.C. American Library Association, 1965.
>
> *Freedom to Read Statement.* Prepared by the Westchester Conference of ALA and the American Book Publishers Council, May 25, 1953. Revised January 28, 1972.
>
> *How Libraries Can Resist Censorship.* Adopted by the ALA Council, Feb. 1, 1962, revised January 28, 1972.
>
> *Media Programs: District and School.* American Library Association and the Association for Educational Communications and Technology, 1975.
>
> *Newsletter on Intellectual Freedom.* A bimonthly publication available by subscription. $5.00 per year. American

Library Association, 50 East Huron Street, Chicago, IL. 60611.

Policies and Procedures for Selection of Instructional Materials. Approved by the American Association of School Librarians Board of Directors at the Mid-Winter Conference of the ALA, 1970.

Resolutions on Challenged Materials. Adopted June 25, 1971, by the ALA Council.

School Library Bill of Rights for School Library Media Center Programs. Approved by the AASL Board of Directors, June, 1969.

Students' Right to Read: 1972 Edition. National Council of Teachers of English, 1111 Kenyon Raod, Urbana, IL. 61801. (Stock No. 20809)

SELECTION POLICY OF
LIBRARY MEDIA CENTERS
USD 353

TABLE OF CONTENTS

Wellington Public Schools
Unified School District 353
Wellington, Kansas
March, 1975

Section 1:

EDUCATIONAL PHILOSOPHY

We, of the schools of Wellington Unified District No. 353 of Sumner County, Kansas, believe:

That our primary function is to train the youth of our community and to help them to achieve the personal development necessary for enlightened adult participation in our democracy.

That we should recognize and respect such individual differences in children as pupil interest, scholastic aptitude, achievement in basic skills, degree of mastery of study skills, special aptitudes, physical and mental health, personality traits, background experience, and personal goals and aspirations for adult life.

That we should recognize the spiritual values of life and should work to instill in youth the intellectual and moral stamina to face life's constant challenge.

That among our major purposes shall be the following:

A. To give all pupils functional training, commensurate with their abilities to learn, in general education areas including communication in written and oral English, basic literature and social studies, fundamental computations, and the rudiments of science.

B. To present opportunities of discovery and suitable preparation to those who wish to develop specific interests, talents, or capacities in the field of fine arts, journalism, the languages, science, mathematics, the industrial arts, home arts, business education, social studies, health and physical education, and athletics.

C. To stimulate the desire and to set the habit for acquiring further knowledge, and within the limits of the capacities and personalities of the candidates, to encourage and assist their meeting the entrance requirements of higher institutions of learning.

D. To give additional basic vocational preparation in various subject areas to those who find it necessary or advisable upon graduation to enter immediately into the fields of business, industry, agriculture, or the armed forces.

E. To provide extensive guidance services in conjunction with re-
    medial types of therapy, forms of individualized education, and
    personal attention. This will enable the young person to under-
    stand himself, to work for self-improvement by learning habits
    of work and play, and to evaluate numerous alternatives open
    to him, so that he may learn self-organization and self-direction
    and practice self-discipline in a manner commendable to him-
    self, his family, his school, and his community.

F. To give pupils real experiences in good citizenship situations in
    which they are made aware of their responsibilities as well as
    their rewards. The situations should also involve respecting the
    rights and opinions of others and acquiring the ideals and per-
    sonal convictions basic to successful citizenship in our American
    democracy.

G. To guide pupils toward constructive attitudes of physical and
    mental health with a consciousness of social and moral issues
    considered basic in acquiring the "good life" in a Christian
    nation.

H. To establish a close-working relationship with parents and
    other adults and with other institutions, using community re-
    sources in such a manner that both the pupil and the commu-
    nity may be served to the end that the greatest direct and in-
    direct returns from the money and time invested will result
    from our educational program.

SCHOOL LIBRARY BILL OF RIGHTS

School libraries are concerned with generating understanding of
American freedoms and with the preservation of these freedoms
through the development of informed and responsible citizens. To
this end the American Association of School Librarians reaffirms the
Library Bill of Rights of the American Library Association and asserts
that the responsibility of the school library is:

To provide materials that will enrich and support the curriculum,
taking into consideration the varied interest, abilities, and maturity
levels of the pupils served.

To provide materials that will stimulate growth in factual knowledge, literary appreciation, aesthetic values, and ethical standards.

To provide a background of information which will enable pupils to
make intelligent judgments in their daily life.

To provide materials on opposing sides of controversial issues so that young citizens may develop under guidance the practice of critical reading and thinking.

To provide materials representative of the many religious, ethnic and cultural groups and their contributions to our American heritage.

To place principle above personal opinion and reason above prejudice in the selection of materials of the highest quality in order to assure a comprehensive collection appropriate for the users of the library.

POLICIES AND PROCEDURES FOR SELECTION OF SCHOOL LIBRARY MEDIA CENTER MATERIALS UNIFIED SCHOOL DISTRICT 353

PATTERNS OF POLICY MAKING—The governing body of the school, the Wellington Board of Education, USD 353, is legally responsible for all matters relating to the operation of the schools. It is recommended that assumption of responsibility and the delegation of authority be stated in a formal policy adopted by the legally responsible body.

SELECTION BY PERSONNEL—Materials for the school library media centers shall be selected by professional personnel in consultation with administration, faculty, students, and parents. Final decision on purchase shall rest with professional personnel in accordance with the formally adopted policy.

TYPES OF MATERIALS COVERED—Criteria are established for all types of materials included in the collection of the library media center.

OBJECTIVES OF SELECTION—The primary objective of a school library media center is to implement, enrich, and support the educational program of the school. Other objectives are concerned with: (1) the development of reading skill, literary taste, discrimination in choice of materials, and (2) instruction in the use of books and libraries.

The school library media center shall contribute to development of the social, intellectual, and spiritual values of the students.

In formulating our policies we considered these subjects which have been areas of controversy:

A. Religion—Factual, unbiased material which represents all major religions should be included in the collection.

B. Ideologies—The library media center shall make available basic factual information of the philosophy which exerts a strong force, either favorable or unfavorable in government, current events, politics, education, or any other phase of life.

C. Profanity and sex—Materials representing accents on sex should be subject to a stern test of literary merit and reality by the librarian who takes into account her reading public. While we would not include the overdramatic or the sensational, the fact of sexual incidents or profanity appearing in a book shall not automatically disqualify it for selection. The decision is to be made on the basis of whether circumstances are realistically dealt with, and whether the book is of literary value. Factual materials of an educational nature on the level of the reading public must be included in the library media center collection.

SELECTION TOOLS—Reputable, unbiased, professionally prepared selection aids shall be consulted by librarians as guides.

CHALLENGED MATERIALS—A procedure shall be established for consideration of criticism of materials by individuals or groups. The School Library Bill of Rights, endorsed by the Council of the American Library Association is basic to this procedure.

A POLICY ON SELECTION OF LIBRARY MEDIA CENTER MATERIALS

The library media center collections are developed systematically to serve a definite teaching function. The collections must be well balanced and well rounded to cover all subjects, types of materials and to offer variety of content.

Qualitative standards for the selection of materials are necessary.

All materials are carefully evaluated before purchase and only materials of good quality are secured. Established criteria for the evaluation and selection of materials are used. Standard tools and reliable guides are used.

Teachers within a particular building are requested and urged to make recommendations for purchase. The teacher plays an important part in the selection of materials for the school library media center, just as the librarian may relate to the teacher information about new materials in the teacher's field. The teacher evaluates materials on the basis of the criteria established for materials in his teaching area. He should be familiar with standard tools and guides.

Students are encouraged to make suggestions for materials to be acquired by the school library media center.

The collections are continuously evaluated in relation to changing curriculum content, new instructional methods, and current needs of teachers and students. Outmoded materials are replaced with those that are up to date, materials no longer useful are discarded and those in poor repair are replaced or repaired.

Acquisitions shall not be limited to annual or semiannual orders but purchased throughout the year as needed.

Administrators, classroom and special teachers, and the library staff endorse and apply the principles incorporated in the School Library Bill of Rights of the American Association of School Librarians, and in any statements for the selection of library materials that school librarians have helped to formulate for the state or for local school system.

BASIC PRINCIPLES FOR THE SELECTION OF MATERIALS FOR THE UNIFIED SCHOOL DISTRICT 353 SCHOOL LIBRARY MEDIA CENTERS

It is the policy of the USD 353 to select materials for our library media centers in accordance with the following:

1. Books and other reading materials shall be chosen for values of interest and enlightenment of all the students of the community. A book shall not be excluded because of the race, nationality, or the political or religious views of the writer.

2. There shall be the fullest practical provision of material presenting all points of view concerning the problems and issues of our times, international, national, and local; and books and other reading matter

CITIZENS' REQUEST FOR RECONSIDERATION
OF A BOOK OR MATERIAL

Author _____

Title _____

Publisher (if known) _____

Request initiated by _____

Telephone _____ Address _____

City _____ Zone _____

Complainant represents

_____ himself/herself

_____ (name organization) _____

_____ (identify other group) _____

1. To what book do you object? (Please be specific; cite pages)

_____

2. What do you feel might be the result of reading this book?

_____

3. For what age group would you recommend this book?

4. Is there anything good about this book?

5. Did you read the entire book? _____ What parts?

6. Are you aware of the judgment of this book by literary critics?

7. What do you believe is the theme of this book?

8. What would you like to do about this book, or ask that your school do?

_____ do not assign it to my child

_____ withdraw it from all students as well as my child

_____ send it back to the English department for reevaluation, or send it
to another department within the school

9. In its place, what book of equal literary quality would you recommend
that would convey as valuable a picture and perspective of our
civilization?

Signature of Complainant

I have read all attached material on selection of materials for the library
media centers of USD 353, Wellington.

Signature of Complainant

---

of sound factual authority shall not be proscribed or removed from
library shelves because of partisan or doctrinal disapproval.

3. Censorship of materials shall be challenged in order to maintain
the school's responsibility to provide information and enlightenment.

Interpreting these principles in selections of materials more specifically, the following will apply:

1. We believe it is the right and responsibility of teachers and librarians to select materials which are carefully balanced to include
various points of view on any controversial subject.

2. Since materials are selected to provide for the interest and need
of the school community and the school program, therefore, they will
be selected cooperatively by teachers, principals, and librarians, sometimes with the assistance of students.

3. Selection of materials will be assisted by the reading, examination, and checking of standard evaluation aids; i.e., standard cata-
logues and book selection aids.

4. Two basic factors, truth and art, will be considered in selection
of materials. This first is factual accuracy, authoritativeness, balance,
and integrity. The second is a quality of stimulating presentation,
imagination, vision, creativeness, style appropriate to the idea, vitality,
and distinction.

5. Materials will be selected in which the presentation and the subject matter are suitable for the grade and interest level at which they
are to be used. They will be considered in relation to both the curriculum and to the personal interest of pupils and teachers.

Books and materials meeting the above standards and principles will
not be banned but books or materials of an obscene nature or those

advocating overthrow of the government of the United States by force or revolution shall not be recommended for purchase.

Criticism of materials that are in the libraries shall be submitted in writing to the Superintendent of Schools. The Board of Education will be informed. Allegations thus submitted will be considered by a committee named by the Board of Education. Appeals from this decision may be made through the Superintendent to the Board of Education for final decision.

Notes

1. American Library Association. Committee on Library Terminology. A.L.A., *Glossary of Library Terms, with a Selection of Terms in Related Fields*, edited by Elizabeth H. Thompson. (Chicago: American Library Association, 1943), p. 122.
2. American Library Association, and Association for Educational Communications and Technology. *Media Programs: District and School* (Chicago: American Library Association, 1975).
3. Ibid.

Selection Aids for the Media Specialist
Bibliography of Selection Sources

GENERAL:

A Basic Book Collection for High Schools. 7th ed. Compiled by Eileen F. Noonan, with the assistance of consultants from A.L.A., A.S.C.D, and N.E.A. Department of Classroom Teachers, N.C.S.S., N.C.T.E., and N.S.T.A. Chicago: American Library Association, 1963.

A Basic Book Collection for Junior High Schools. Compiled by Margaret V. Spengler. 3rd ed. Chicago: American Library Association, 1960.

The Booklist. Chicago: American Library Association, published twice monthly, latest issues.

Books for Junior College Libraries. James W. Pirie, compiler. Chicago: American Library Association, latest.

Choice: Books for College Libraries. Association of Colleges and

Research Libraries. Middletown, Connecticut: Association of Colleges and Research Libraries, American Library Association, 11 issues yearly.

Junior High School Library Catalog, 1974. New York: H. W. Wilson, 1974, with supplements.

Senior High School Library Catalog, 1977. New York: H. W. Wilson, 1977, with supplements.

SPECIFIC REFERENCE SOURCES:

American History Booklist for High Schools: A Selection of Supplementary Readings. Edited by Ralph and Marian Brown, with the assistance of Martin L. Fausold; Ellis A. Johnson; and William G. Tyrrell. Washington, D.C.: National Council for the Social Studies, 1969.

American Library Association. *Let's Read Together: Books for Family Enjoyment.* 3rd ed. Selected and annotated by a Special Committee of the National Congress of Parents and Teachers and the Children's Services Division, A.L.A. Chicago: American Library Association, 1969.

American Library Association, and Association for Educational Communications and Technology. *Media Programs: District and School.* Chicago: American Library Association, 1975.

Asia Society. *Asia: A Guide to Paperbacks.* Rev. ed. by Ainslie T. Embree. New York: The Society, 1968.

Audiovisual Marketplace: A Multi-Media Guide. New York: Bowker, annual.

Bertalan, Frank J. *The Junior College Library Collection.* General Editor, Frank J. Bertalan. Newark, N.J.: Bro-Dart Foundation, 1970.

Book Review Digest. New York: H. W. Wilson, annual.

Books for Youth: A Guide for Teen-Age Readers. Edited by Catherine C. Robertson, and others. 4th ed. Toronto: Toronto Public Library, 1972.

Books in American History: A Basic Book List for High Schools. Edited by John E. Wiltz. Bloomington, Ind.: Indiana University Press, 1964.

California Library Association. Young Adult Librarians' Round

Table. *A Subject List of Historical Fiction for Young Adult Reading*. Sacramento: The Association, 1964.

Carter, Yvonne; Jones, Milbrey L; Moses, Kathlyn J.; Sutherland, Louise V.; and Watt, Lois B. *Aids to Media Selection for Students and Teachers*. Washington, D.C.: U.S. Department of Health, Education, and Welfare, 1972.

Carlsen, Robert G. *Books and The Teen-Age Reader*. 2nd ed. New York: Bantam, 1980.

Chapman, Abraham. *The Negro in American Literature and a Bibliography of Literature by and about Negro Americans*. Madison, Wis.: Wisconsin Council of Teachers of English, 1966.

Cheney, Frances Neel. *Fundamental Reference Sources*. Chicago: American Library Association, 1971.

The Committee on College Reading. *Good Reading: A Helpful Guide for Serious Readers*. Prepared by The Committee on College Reading, J. Sherwood Weber, editor; Anna Rothe, assistant editor. New York: New American Library, frequently revised.

Courtney, Winifred F., ed. *The Reader's Adviser: A Guide to the Best in Literature*. New York: Bowker, 1968– .

Deason, Hilary J. *The AAAS Science Book List*. 3d ed. A selected and annotated list of science and mathematics books for secondary school students, college undergraduates, and nonspecialists. Washington, D.C.: American Association for the Advancement of Science, 1970.

Deason, Hilary J. *The AAAS Science Book List for Children*. 3d ed. Washington, D.C.: American Association for the Advancement of Science, 1972.

Dickinson, A. T. *American Historical Fiction*. 3d ed. Edited by A. T. Dickinson, Jr. Metuchen, N.J.: Scarecrow Press, 1971.

Dobler, Lavinia., ed. *The Dobler World Directory of Youth Periodicals*. 3d. enl. ed. Compiled and edited by Lavinia Dobler and Muriel Fuller. New York: Citation Press, 1970.

Dodds, Barbara. *Negro Literature for High School Students*. Champaign, Ill.: National Council of Teachers of English, 1968.

Dunlap, Joseph R. *Debate Index, 2d Supplement*. Compiled by Joseph R. Dunlap and Martin A. Kuhn. New York: H. W. Wilson, 1964.

Eakin, Mary K. *Subject Index to Books for Intermediate Grades.* 3d ed. Chicago: American Library Association, 1963.

Educational Film Library Association. *Film Evaluation Guide: Supplement Two.* New York: The Association, 1972.

Edwards, Margaret A. *The Fair Garden and the Swarm of Beasts: The Library and the Young Adult.* Rev. and expanded. New York: Hawthorn Books, 1974.

El-Hi Textbooks in Print. New York: Bowker, annual.

Enoch Pratt Free Library. *Reference Books: A Guide for Students and Other Users of the Library.* Baltimore, The Library, latest.

Fader, Daniel N. *Hooked on Books: Program and Proof,* by Daniel N. Fader and Elton B. McNeil. New York: Putnam, 1968.

Farrell, Robert V., comp. *Latin American: Books for High Schools: An Annotated Bibliography.* Compiled by Robert V. Farrell and John F. Hohenstein; edited by Karna S. Wilgus. New York: Center for International Relations, 1969.

Fiction Catalog. 9th ed. Edited by Estelle A. Fidell. New York: H.W. Wilson, 1975, with supplements.

4000 Books for Secondary School Libraries: A Basic List. Compiled by the Library Committee of the National Association of Independent Schools. New York: Bowker, 1968.

Films for Young Adults: A Selected List. Prepared by The New York Library Association, Children's and Young Adult Services Section. New York: Library Association, 1966.

Forrester, Gertrude. *Occupational Literature: An Annotated Bibliography.* New York: H.W. Wilson, 1971.

High Interest—Easy Reading: For Junior and Senior High School Students. 2d ed. New York: Citation Press, 1972.

Irwin, Leonard B., comp. *A Guide to Historical Fiction: For the Use of Schools, Libraries and the General Reader.* 10th rev. ed. Brooklawn, N.J.: McKinley, 1971.

Irwin, Leonard B., comp. *A Guide to Historical Reading: Nonfiction; For the Use of Schools, Libraries and the General Reader.* 9th rev. ed. Brooklawn, N.J.: McKinley, 1970.

Johnson, Harry Alleyn. *Multimedia Materials for Afro-American Studies: A Curriculum Orientation and Annotated Bibliography of Resources.* Edited and compiled by Harry Alleyn Johnson. New York: Bowker, 1971.

Katz, Bill, comp. *Magazines for Libraries: For the General Reader and Public, School, Junior College and College Libraries,* by Bill Katz and Barry Gargal, science editor. New York: Bowker, 1972.

Katz, Bill, comp. *Teacher's Guide to American Negro History.* Chicago: Quadrangle Books, 1968.

Lepman, Jella. *Bridge of Children's Books.* Translated from the German by Edith McCormick. Chicago: American Library Association, 1969.

The Literature of Jazz. Compiled by Donald Kennington. Chicago: American Library Association, 1971.

Logasa, Hannah. *Historical Fiction: An Annotated Bibliography, Guide for Senior and Junior High Schools, and Colleges.* 9th rev. and enl. ed. Brooklawn, N.J.: McKinley, 1968.

Logasa, Hannah. *Science for Youth: An Annotated Bibliography for Children and Young Adults.* Brooklawn, N.J.: McKinley, 1967.

Mapp, Edward. *Books for Occupational Education Programs: A List for Community Colleges, Technical Institutes and Vocational Schools.* New York: Bowker, 1971.

McGraw-Hill Basic Bibliography of Science and Technology; recent titles on more than 7,000 subjects. Compiled and annotated by the editors of the *McGraw-Hill Encyclopedia of Science and Technology.* New York: McGraw, 1966.

Mersand, Joseph. *Index to Plays.* Metuchen, N.J.: Scarecrow Press, 1966.

The Mindbenders: Alcohol, Drugs, Narcotics, LSD. Selected and prepared by the Young Adult Services, Prince George's County Memorial Library. Upper Marlboro, Md.: Prince George's County Memorial Library, 1966.

Multimedia Approach to Children's Literature: A Selective List of Films, Filmstrips and Recordings Based on Children's Books, by Ellin Greene and Madalynne Schoenfeld. Chicago: American Library Association, 1972.

National Center for Audio Tapes. Boulder, Colo.: University of Colorado, 197– (latest).

National Council of Teachers of English, Committee on College and Adult Reading List. *The College and Adult Reading List of Books in Literature and the Fine Arts.* Edward Lueders, editorial chairman. New York: Washington Square Press, 1962.

National Information Center for Educational Media. *Index to Black History and Studies.* Washington, D.C.: The Center, 1971.

National Information Center for Educational Media. *Index to Ecology* (multimedia). Washington, D.C.: The Center, 1971.

The Negro American in Paperback: A Selected List of Paperbound Books Compiled and Annotated for Secondary School Students, by Joseph E. Penn; Elaine C. Brooks, and Mollie L. Berch. Washington, D.C.: National Education Association, 1967.

New York Library Association. Children's and Young Adult Services Section. *Records and Cassettes for Young Adults: A Selected List.* New York: The Association, 1972.

New York Public Library. Office of Young Adult Services *Books for the Teen Age.* New York, annual compilation.

Notable Children's Books, 1974, 1975 Chicago: American Library Association.

Outstanding Biographies for the College Bound Student. Chicago: American Library Association, most recent.

Outstanding Books on the Now Scene for the College Bound Student. Chicago: American Library Association, most recent.

Outstanding Fiction for the College Bound. Chicago: American Library Association, most recent.

Outstanding Non-Fiction for the College Bound Student. Chicago: American Library Association, most recent.

Outstanding Theater for the College Bound. Chicago: American Library Association, most recent.

Paperback Books for Young People: An Annotated Guide to Publishers and Distributors, By John T. Gillespie and Diana L. Spirt. Chicago: American Library Association, 1972.

The Paperback Goes to School: A Selected List of Elementary and Secondary-School Titles. Selected by a committee of the National Education Association; the American Association of School Librarians; and the National Council of Teachers of English. Washington, D.C.: National Education Association, 1973.

Pearson, Mary D. *Recordings in the Public Library*. Chicago: American Library Association, 1963.

Perkins, Flossie L. *Book and Non-Book Media: Annotated Guide to Selection Aids for Educational Materials*. Urbana, Ill.: National Council of Teachers of English, 1972.

Pirie, James W., comp. *Books for Junior College Libraries*. Chicago: American Library Association, 1969.

Pohle, Linda C. *A Guide to Popular Government Publications for Libraries and Home Reference*. Littleton, Colo.: Libraries Unlimited, 1972.

Porter, Dorothy B. *The Negro in the United States: A Selected Bibliography*. Washington, D.C.: Library of Congress (for sale by Superintendent of Documents), 1970.

Public Library Catalog. 6th ed. (1973). Edited by Gary L. Bogart and Estelle A. Fidell. New York: H. W. Wilson, 1974.

Raab, Joseph A. *Audiovisual Materials in Mathematics*. Washington, D.C.: National Council of Teachers of Mathematics, 1971.

Reading Ladders for Human Relations. 5th ed. Virginia M. Reid, editor, and the Committee on Reading for Human Relations of the National Council of Teachers of English. Washington, D.C.: American Council on Education, 1972.

Recommended Materials for a Professional Library in the School. Michigan Association of School Librarians, University of Michigan. Ann Arbor, Mich.: The Association, 1962.

Reference Books for Small and Medium-Sized Public Libraries. Committee of the Reference Services Division. Chicago: American Library Association, 1969.

Requa, Eloise G. *The Developing Nations*. Detroit: Gale Research Co., 1965.

Rosenberg, Judith K. *Young People's Literature in Series: Fiction; an annotated bibliographical guide,* by Judith K. Rosenberg and Kenyon C. Rosenberg. Littleton, Colo.; Libraries Unlimited, 1972.

Rosenberg, Judith K. *Young People's Literature in Series: Publishers' and Non-Fiction Series; an annotated bibliographical guide*. Littleton, Colo.: Libraries Unlimited, 1973.

Rufsvold, Margaret I. *Guides to Educational Media: Films, Filmstrips, Kinescopes, Phonodiscs, Phototapes, Programmed Instruc-*

tion Materials, Slides, Transparencies, Videotapes. 3d ed. Chicago: American Library Association, 1971.

Schaaf, William L. *The High School Mathematics Library.* Washington, D.C.: National Council of Teachers of Mathematics, 1970.

Schuman, Patricia. *Materials for Occupational Education: An Annotated Source Guide.* New York: Bowker, 1971.

Science for Society: A Bibliography. Prepared by the editor of the Commission on Science Education, American Association for the Advancement of Science. Washington, D.C.: American Association for the Advancement of Science, 1974.

Scott, Marian H. *Periodicals for School Libraries: A Guide To Magazines, Newspapers and Periodical Indexes.* Chicago: American Library Association, 1969.

Sell, Violet. *Subject Index to Poetry for Children and Young People,* by Violet Sell; Dorothy B. Birzzell Smith; Ardis Sarff O Hoyt; and Mildred Bakke, compilers. Chicago: American Library Association, 1967.

Sheehy, Eugene P. *Guide to Reference Books.* 9th ed. Chicago: American Library Association, 1976.

Sheehy, Eugene P. *Guide to Reference Books, 8th edition. First Supplement.* Chicago: American Library Association, 1968.

Sheehy, Eugene P. *Guide to Reference Books, 8th edition. Second Supplement.* Chicago: American Library Association, 1970.

Sheehy, Eugene P. *Guide to Reference Books, 8th edition. Third Supplement.* Chicago: American Library Association, 1972.

Smith, Lillian H. *The Unreluctant Years: A Critical Approach to Children's Literature.* Chicago: American Library Association, 1953.

Spache, George D. *Good Reading for the Disadvantaged Reader; Multi-ethnic Resources.* New York: Garrard, 1970.

Stensland, Anna Lee. *Literature By and About the American Indians: An Annotated Bibliography for Junior and Senior High Students.* Urbana, Ill.: National Council of Teachers of English, 1973.

Subject Guide to Major United States Government Publications, by Ellen Jackson. Chicago: American Library Association, 1968.

Taggart, Dorothy T. *A Guide to Sources in Educational Media and Technology*. Metuchen, N.J.: Scarecrow Press, 1975.

The Teacher's Library: How to Organize It and What to Include. Washington, D.C.: National Education Association, 1966.

Walker, Elinor. *Book Bait: Detailed Notes on Adult Books Popular with Young People*. Chicago: American Library Association, 1969.

Walker, Elinor. *Doors to More Mature Reading*. Chicago: American Library Association, 1964.

Walsh, S. Padraig., comp. *General Encyclopedias in Print, 1968: A Comparative Analysis*. New York: Bowker, 1968.

Wynar, Bohdan S. *Reference Books in Paperback: An Annotated Guide*. Littleton, Colo.: Libraries Unlimited, 1972.

Wynar, Christine L. *Guide to Reference Books for School Media Centers*. Littleton, Colo.: Libraries Unlimited, 1973.

Young Phenomenon: Paperbacks in our Schools, by John T. Gillespie and Diana L. Spirt. Chicago: American Library Association, 1972.

PERIODICALS USEFUL IN SELECTION:

American Libraries. 11 issues. Single copies of available back issues, $2.00. Subscription price is included in American Library Association dues. Available on paid subscription to libraries at $20 per year. Chicago: American Library Association.

Audiovisual Instruction. 10 issues. Goes to all members of the Association for Educational Communications and Technology. Annual subscription $18.00. Washington, D.C.: Association for Educational Communications and Technology.

The Booklist. 23 issues, twice monthly except one in August. $20.00 per year. Single copies of available back issues $1.00. Chicago: American Library Association.

Choice. 11 issues. $35.00 per year. Chicago: American Library Association.

The English Journal. Monthly. Urbana, Ill.: National Council of Teachers of English.

Teacher. Monthly, 77 Bedford St., Stamford, CT 06901 Macmillan Professional Magazines, Inc.

Instructor. Monthly. Instructor Park, Dansville, N.Y.: Instructor Publications, Inc.

School Media Quarterly. Four times yearly. Single copies $2.00. Journal of the American Association of School Librarians. Sent regularly to division members only. Not available by subscription. Chicago: American Library Association.

Top of the News. Quarterly. $15.00 per year, single copies $3.75. Journal of the Children's Services Division and Young Adult Services Division. Sent to division members. Chicago: American Library Association.

For Further Reading

Bomar, Cora Paul. *Guide to the Development of Educational Media Selection Centers,* by Cora Paul Bomar; M. Ann Heidbreder; and Carol A. Nemeyer. Chicago: American Library Association, 1973.

Brown, James W. *Administering Educational Media,* by James W. Brown and Kenneth D. Norberg. New York: McGraw-Hill, 1973.

Cleary, Florence Damon. *Blueprints for Better Reading: School Programs for Promoting Skill and Interest in Reading.* 2d ed. New York: H.W. Wilson, 1972.

Davies, Ruth Ann. *The School Library: A Force for Educational Excellence.* New York: Bowker, 1973.

Edwards, Margaret A. *The Fair Garden and the Swarm of Beasts: The Library and the Young Adult.* Rev. ed. New York: Hawthorn Books, 1974.

Erickson, W.H. *Administering Instructional Media Programs.* New York: Macmillan, 1968.

Galin, Saul. *Reference Books: How to Select and Use Them,* by Saul Galin and Peter Spielberg. New York: Random House, 1969.

Gaver, Mary V. *The Elementary School Library Collection.* (Williamsport, Pa. Bro-dart, annual).

Gaver, Mary V. *Services of Secondary School Media Centers: Evaluation and Development.* (Chicago: American Library Association, 1971.)

Gillespie, John T. *Paperback Books for Young People: An Annotated Guide to Publishers and Distributors,* by John T. Gillespie and Diana L. Spirt. Chicago: American Library Association, 1972.

Guide to Instructional Materials. Madison, Wis.: Demco Educational Corporation, 1973.

Guide to the Selection of Books and Media for Your Secondary School Library. Momence, Ill.: Baker & Taylor Company, annual, with supplements.

Haviland, Virginia., ed. *Children's Books of International Interest.* Chicago: American Library Association, 1972.

Hinman, Dorothy. *Reading for Boys and Girls: Illinois,* by Dorothy Hinman and Ruth Zimmerman, for the Illinois State Library. Chicago: American Library Association, 1970.

Hodges, Elizabeth D. *Books for Elementary School Libraries: An Initial Collection.* Chicago: American Library Association, 1969.

Merritt, LeRoy Charles. *Book Selection and Intellectual Freedom.* New York: H.W. Wilson, 1970.

Munson, Amelia H. *An Ample Field: Books and Young People.* Chicago: American Library Association, 1950.

National Association of Independent Schools. *Books for Secondary School Libraries.* New York: Bowker, 1971.

New Educational Materials: A Classified Guide. New York: Citation Press, annual.

Perkins, Ralph. *Book Selection Media.* National Council of Teachers of English, 1967.

The Right to Read and the Nation's Libraries, edited by the Right to Read Committees of the American Association of School Librarians and Children's Services Division, Public Library Association. Chicago: American Library Association, 1974.

Rowell, John. *Educational Media Selection Centers: Identification and Analysis of Current Practices,* by John Rowell and M. Ann Heidbreder. Chicago: American Library Association, 1971.

Saunders, Helen E. *The Modern School Library: Its Administration as a Materials Center.* Metuchen, N.J.: Scarecrow Press, 1968.

Sullivan, Peggy., ed. *Realization: The Final Report of the Knapp School Libraries Project.* Chicago: American Library Association, 1968.

White, Carl M. *Sources of Information in the Social Sciences: A Guide to the Literature.* 2d rev. ed. Chicago: American Library Association, 1973.

VI
Acquisition and Ordering
of Materials for the
Library Media Center

"Acquisitions work in a library is the means by which additions are made to the library's collection."[1] The acquisition department is defined as "the administrative unit in charge of selecting and acquiring books, periodicals, and other material by purchase, exchange and gift, and of keeping the necessary records of these additions. Sometimes referred to as Order Department or Accession Department."[2] In the school media center, as in any library, it is an important function. The ordering and receiving of all types of materials must be systematically organized; records including copies of purchase orders, invoices, materials which are "on order" or "in process" must be noted in files, accompanied by any correspondence in relation to such orders.

Verification and Search of Information for Purchase

For the library media center with a large and growing collection it is important that requests for purchase be checked before ordering to ascertain whether the center may already have the specified materials; to compare prices for purchase; and to consider the balance of the collection. The material must be in print or available; incorrect or incomplete information may have been given in the order request.

Verification of the order request information is accomplished with the standard selection aids and bibliographic tools which are considered authoritative. (See Chapter 5). Information may be added, or in some cases, deleted from the order file. If printed cards are to be ordered, further information is often needed. The card catalog and shelf list will indicate whether or not the library media center already has the materials requested for ordering. As an "ordered" file is maintained, this should also be checked so as not to reorder materials which are "on order" for the library. The "processing" file must be checked in the same way. Not only the beginner, who does not know the collection well, but the experienced media specialist will appreciate the value of search and verification before ordering. One cannot rely on memory as the collection grows.

Some sources for verification of books (titles, authors, publishers, etc.):

> *Union Catalog* (when available)
> *Publishers Weekly*
> Standard Catalogs of H. W. Wilson Company *(Senior High Catalog, Junior High Catalog, Children's Catalog, Fiction Catalog*
> *Books in Print*

The library should own an up-to-date copy of *Books In Print*. It is considered the most comprehensive source to check whether a book is in print and to obtain other data. Some books are not included but those from the majority of regular publishers are; a book not listed in the latest *Books in Print* is often not available.

Nonbook materials and the increasing number of interesting and useful specialized books from alternative, small, and organizational publishers are more difficult to verify. Helpful finding tools for these materials include:

Blue Book of Audiovisual Materials. Educational Screen and
    Audiovisual Guide, annual
Sources: A Guide to Print and Nonprint Materials. Neal Schu-
    man Publishers, Inc. Three times a year.
Audiovisual Instruction. Monthly publication of the As-
    sociation for Educational Communication and
    Technology.

For both book and nonbook materials a file of catalogs and
announcements from publishers and producers should be
maintained, as well as the catalogs from the jobbers who supply
all materials, both book and nonbook. Outstanding catalogs
from school districts which list the collection in that district are
also a good source for identifying and verifying materials. In
a time when prices are often changing, the publisher's catalogs
are the most up to date source for prices of materials.

Verification of periodicals can be made through the jobber
or subscription agency, but a source which the media center
will find invaluable is: Scott, Marian H. *Periodicals for School Libraries: A Guide to Magazines, Newspapers and Periodical Indexes,*
revised edition. (Chicago: American Library Association, 1973).
It is most comprehensive and gives full information. A permanent up-to-date collection of periodicals is most important
on the secondary level. It is wise to maintain files of most magazines indexed in *The Readers' Guide to Periodical Literature* and
for such files to be on a twelve-month basis.

Other sources for verification of periodicals include:

Ayer's Directory of Newspapers, Magazines and Trade Publications
Ulrich's International Periodicals Directory
Access, The Supplementary Index to Periodicals

For the purchase of pamphlets it is wise to verify purchase
in the *Vertical File Index,* published by H. W. Wilson Company.
It is the best source and is published monthly. Pamphlets are
not usually listed in *Books in Print* nor in *Cumulative Book Index*
nor in the standard catalogs of the H. W. Wilson Company,

and again *Sources* is extremely useful here. Requests for purchase should be checked just as books or other media are checked, insofar as possible. A form letter can be used when, upon occasion, it is necessary to contact the publisher directly.

Consideration of Centralized Processing

Centralized processing may be defined as the handling in one library or central agency of all the procedures necessary to prepare material for shelving and use in the library media center. It is defined as "The administrative unit in charge of cataloging, classification and the physical preparation of books for the shelves (to include all materials in the modern media center), and, in some libraries, of other routines, as order work, accessioning and inventorying. The term Processing Department is sometimes used." (Thompson, Elizabeth H., *A.L.A. Glossary of Library Terms with a Selection of Terms in Related Fields.*)[3]

Where there are two or more schools in a system or district, centralized processing should certainly be considered. When there is centralized processing the requests for materials which have been selected and verified are submitted to the technical services or processing department to be ordered. Centralized ordering and processing has many advantages for the individual school library media center. Whether the processing is by single media center or by a centralized agency within the district the process must be organized and routine. In most cases, processing at the single school level is inefficient and duplicative, and a poor use of professional time. Its advantage is that the media specialist does know the collection much better than when someone else catalogs the materials. The cataloging is apt to be tailored specifically to the uses to which the catalog is put in that particular school and, in many cases, is more accurate and complete.

Advantages of centralized processing are many and persuasive and include: the fact that the media specialist is free for guidance and work with students and teachers and need not spend so much time at technical organizational tasks; that the processing of large orders is more economical and efficient as card-production units can be utilized to reduce production time; that business routines are simplified for the district. This will result in uniformity in cataloging and classification for the schools within the district, but not everyone will be entirely satisfied with the results. Compromises are necessary whenever there is centralized processing, and the cataloging idiosyncracies of some individuals must yield, but it is worth it.

Consideration of Commercial Cataloging

For the smaller school district where there is no possibility of centralized processing, there are alternative approaches to consider. Commercial cataloging is recommended; it is available at reasonable prices from a number of companies, including jobbers. It has advantages as well as some disadvantages. Cataloging from various jobbers and for various types of materials will not be uniform, may not be in the format of the rest of the catalog, and may not be as detailed as is needed in the center. Much has been written about commercial cataloging and its advantages for the library media center. The media specialist must weigh priorities, assess staff capabilities and the needs of the students who use the library media center, and decide accordingly in terms of overall program objectives to be served.

Alternative Approaches to Processing: Interlibrary Cooperation

In many parts of the country regional processing centers are functioning well. This is a possibility to consider as the interlibrary, intersystem cooperation of all types of libraries grows throughout the nation. Some schools have become regional centers, providing processing services for schools within the area. Some schools have agreements with regional library systems, while other schools rely on public library systems to handle processing. It may be possible that the media specialist will have to consider and try alternative approaches before arriving at the best means of efficient and thorough processing of all materials for the particular situation.

Order Authority and Accounting

Before any orders are placed the media specialist must know thoroughly the routines and procedures of the school district. The media specialist must have established the budget in detail and a procedure for order authority for the individual media center is usually accomplished through the use of a *purchase order and claim voucher* presented to the business office at the time an order is to be made. The media specialist must have a day-to-day knowledge of how much has been spent out of the budget allocation and how much remains. It is well to have a small portion of money available at the building level in an activities account, for making small purchases, for mailing, and for other petty cash needs such as emergency purchase from the local book store. A procedure should be established for end of fiscal year reporting which will include an audit, either as a separate account or as a part of the local district audit procedure. Before any orders are placed or any funds expended, the media specialist must sit down with the administrator or fiscal officer and establish all procedures for ordering and accounting. (See example of *Purchase Order and Claim Voucher* at the end of this chapter.)

Bidding

Many state education departments as well as many local school districts require that bids be let for purchase of materials, supplies, or equipment. *Formal bidding* is the process of sealed bids from vendors for certain items which are publicly opened on a given date that has been advertised locally. Firms which have proven reliable are invited to submit bids. A list of dealers is usually available from the district offices or from the state department of education. The aim of competitive formal bidding is to get the best goods and services for the money, the most at the lowest possible cost. It is also a guard against vendors who offer special enticements to administrators, librarians, or to districts and against favoritism on the part of the one placing the order. It is also a safeguard against substandard or delinquent service or materials. It gives the vendor or seller an opportunity to sell to an entire district or state. Bidding does have its disadvantages: the possibility of poor service from the vendor, the red tape of negotiation of the contract through the fiscal agency, inaccuracies of billing for a particular library media center. The need for one time or seasonal ordering is another severe handicap of the bidding procedure. Materials often will not be offered for bids until the summer months or the beginning of the fiscal year. Ordering in the media center should be an ongoing procedure, to meet the needs of the center as soon as possible. Many state laws exempt library material from a bid requirement, as do many school districts. Many items purchased for a library are uniquely available from sole source vendors.

Informal bidding is a less formal procedure and indicates that the bids do not have to be advertised. A few firms may be asked, even by telephone, for their prices on an item or items needed. This is widely used as a bidding system by media centers, particularly when expenditure is below $1000. In the case of informal bidding, the district should establish standards of bidding practice to be followed by all employees, including the media specialists.

These guideline should include the following as a part of the informal bidding procedure:

1. Specification. This is particularly important for equipment.
2. Ordering frequency. To set a schedule for anticipated ordering.
3. Quality and condition. To list unacceptable conditions under which materials may be returned; to agree that substitutions and changes in the order will be acceptable.
4. Invoices and packing slips. It is well to request in-

voices in duplicate or triplicate for use in the processing center and to send to the purchasing or administrative office.

5. Time of delivery. Today this varies but it should be
discussed with the vendor or jobber.

6. Return and service policies. The conditions under
which all materials may be returned, may be ordered
on approval, and servicing of all equipment. Conditions of warranty (especially for equipment).

7. Discounts. The media specialist should request a list
by type of material, giving the acceptable discount on
materials. This is more or less standard but should be
reviewed by the media specialist.

8. Payment of charges. Details should be worked out
and understood by both parties before ordering.

9. Services of area representatives. Close contact with
the representative and knowledge of special services
available.

10. Bidding process. In case of bidding, this should be
specific and should provide satisfactory service to the
center, to the business office, and should be realistic
in regard to specifications.

The above are basic considerations in all purchase agreements whether on bid or not.

Where informal bidding is the usual procedure (as it is in
most schools), the media specialist must know the school district's requirements, the laws of the state which exempt particular materials from bid requirements, and the working agreement, which may be formal or informal, by which the media
specialist assumes responsibility for ordering of materials. Each
type of material is unique and many purchasing methods may
be used by the media specialist in the school.

The goal in purchasing whether by formal bid, informal bid,
or by direct order to the publisher is to acquire the best of materials or services with the least cost. It is important to consider
the quality of materials as well as services of the vendor. A
good source to identify suppliers of specific items or materials
is important. These recommended sources are:

The Audiovisual Marketplace. New York, R. R. Bowker, annual.

The Audiovisual Equipment Directory. Washington, D.C.: National Audio-Visual Association, annual.

Audiovisual Source Directory. New York: Motion Pictures Enterprises Publications, Inc., annual.

AV Guide: The Learning Media Magazine. Educational Screen and Audiovisual Guide, monthly.

NICEM Indexes (8 mm motion cartridges, 16 mm educational films, 35 mm educational filmstrips, overhead transparencies). New York: R. R. Bowker, annual.

A Guide to Sources in Educational Media and Technology. Dorothy T. Taggart. Metuchen, N.J.: The Scarecrow Press, Inc., 1975.

The latter bibliography is a listing of sources of information on all media and may be useful to have in the library media center.

Jobbers

The media specialist will order from many sources. A principal supplier of library media center materials will be a "jobber." A "jobber" is defined as a "wholesaler who sells only to schools and institutions rather than to wholesale organizations." Today many of the print-oriented jobbers are stocking and providing nonprint materials as well as print materials. This is a help in simplifying the media center's problems in acquisition. The inexperienced media specialist could read the professional publications and note the advertisements of national and regional suppliers of both book and nonbook materials, confer with others at association and area meetings, and view exhibits of materials whenever possible. A conference or meeting where displays are available is a good opportunity to talk with the representative of the company or the jobber, and check with colleagues about his reputation and performance.

The choosing of the jobber to supply materials to the library media center is very important. The jobber should be evaluated carefully. Some key factors to consider in initially selecting or staying with a jobber are:

1. Percentage of unfilled titles of the order.
2. The length of time for delivery of materials ordered, or for delivery of a part of an order.
3. The reorder service; the quickness and willingness of the jobber to correct mistakes and send replacement copies.
4. Accuracy of shipments and invoicing; the quality of billing and the provision of duplicate invoices as requested.
5. The discounts allowed by the jobber.
6. The courtesy shown the library media center by the jobber.
7. The general integrity of the jobber.

In addition to the jobber there are other possible sources for materials depending on the type of material, when it is needed. Though usually purchased through the jobber or through the publisher or producer, materials will in some cases, be purchased at the local bookstore or at a nearby university bookstore. Many items purchased for the library media center, as we have said, are uniquely available from a sole source vendor (such as an encyclopedia). The best overall plan to follow is for the media director or purchasing agent for the district to have a working agreement with the jobber or vendor for the purchase of the majority of materials. The important consideration is the reputation of the jobber, the integrity of the representative. Making the jobber decision is an important responsibility of the media specialist.

Both in bidding and in direct purchase the amount of discount available from the jobber or supplier, must be considered as well as payment terms. Among the services one should ask for and be able to expect from a jobber are such things as: exhibits for district media personnel and teachers; preview opportunities; catalogs supplied for all school buildings; return or guarantee of materials. Some jobbers have excellent exhibit op-

portunities in various areas of the country where one can examine new materials. These are very useful opportunities for
selection, for communicating with the jobber, and for talking
with other media specialists.

Purchase Orders

A *standing order* is often used in the case of materials which
are published annually (or biannually) and which the library
media center will want on a regular basis. A *standing order* or
continuation order is defined as "a general direction to an agent
or publisher to supply until otherwise notified future numbers
of a continuation as issued."[4] These include serials, annuals,
yearbooks, multivolume sets with yearly or biyearly publications, and sets in series.

The media specialist may request that all future publications
in a certain series come to the center. This can be done by a
standing order. A "blanket order" specifies that the jobber will
ship any new title in a particular subject area or series. This
can be done satisfactorily only in a center with a large budget.
Ordinarily, the library media center will select materials individually as needed, a better procedure because needs change
from year to year. One area of the collection may grow until it
is not advantageous to add to it, and the money should go into
another area of the library resource.

Order Forms

A multicopy requisition form which can be filed is recommended. These can be typed with one of the copies being
shown in the shelf list as an "on order" notification to the library staff in regard to the particular item. Other copies can
be distributed to the business office, the media center file, and
the processing file (when appropriate). (See Addenda to this
chapter.)

A second method for ordering materials is to type a list-form
and to submit one or more copies to the vendor as an order. A

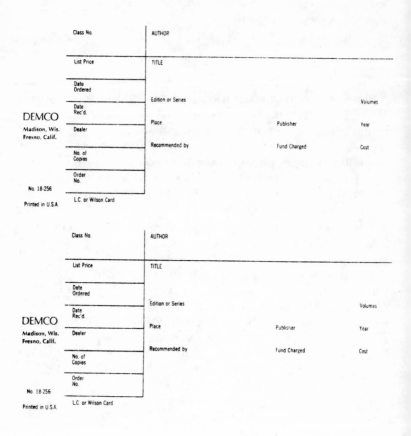

Multicopy Order Forms. Figure 1.

GAYLORD BROS. INC.   NO. 566 - NO CARBON REQUIRED   PRINTED IN USA.

L. C. CARD NUMBER

CLASS NO.	AUTHOR				CARD SETS ORD'D
	TITLE				L.C.
ACC. NO.					
LIST PRICE	PLACE	PUBLISHER		YEAR	L.J.
DEALER	VOLS.	SERIES		EDITION	WI.
NO. OF COPIES	RECOMMENDED BY	DATE ORDERED		COST	OTHER
ORDER NO.	FUND CHARGED	DATE RECEIVED		S.B.N.	

L. C. CARD NUMBER

CLASS NO.	AUTHOR				CARD SETS ORD'D
	TITLE				L.C.
ACC. NO.					
LIST PRICE	PLACE	PUBLISHER		YEAR	L.J.
DEALER	VOLS.	SERIES		EDITION	WI.
NO. OF COPIES	RECOMMENDED BY	DATE ORDERED		COST	OTHER
ORDER NO.	FUND CHARGED	DATE RECEIVED		S.B.N.	

Multicopy Order Forms. Figure 2.

copy (or multiple copies) will be kept on file. The advantage of this method is that the list is a compact record for the library media specialist, however, it cannot be interfiled or filed as card-form copies of the order can be. Information is the same in either method. Billing, shipping, and binding instructions must be included in either case. If out-of-print books are ordered it is best to submit the out-of-print list to one dealer at a time to avoid duplication. This is a good rule to follow in all ordering; to submit orders to one dealer at a time.

Nonbook Materials

Ordering of nonbook materials as discussed previously in this chapter is done in much the same way as is that of books. Most of the nonbook vendors require that their catalog number be used to order either equipment or materials to avoid confusion in fulfillment (largely now computerized.) The word or phrase describing each item should be given along with the title of the item: as *filmstrip, tape, record,* etc. Billing and shipping instructions must be given for all materials, and a copy of the order and all instructions retained. Microfilm will have to be ordered separately.

Periodicals

Periodicals for the school media center are best ordered through a subscription jobber or magazine agency. Some magazines are not supplied by agencies, however, and must be ordered separately.

Individual orders to the publisher may be cheaper, but managing orders for a library media center is difficult, especially if there are more than fifty periodical orders. It is done more efficiently by an agency who will follow up on copies or titles not received. Subscriptions should begin and end at the same time for all titles, if possible, as in August for beginning of the subscription and July for the last issue of the subscription year. The agent should have the order by May. Forms are usually available or a typed form can be used, giving full information: title of periodical, publisher, location, period to be covered, number of copies wanted, cost and renewal information. A copy should be retained by the media specialist. Billing and shipping instructions should be exact and complete.

The media center should maintain a "check-in" file for all periodicals, a card file of all titles the library subscribes to for the year. A card form is available to check as monthly issues (or weekly issues) are received. On-order files are maintained, as well, as they are for other media in the center. Such card files for periodicals should be maintained for at least two years as should correspondence from the vendor. A sample of the card file for both weekly and monthly publications is shown: See *Figure*.

Newspapers

In the school library media center newspapers are ordered only once a year, with few exceptions. The orders should be ready in May with the subscription to begin with the beginning of the school year to last throughout the year. Information should include the title of the newspaper wanted, the publisher's name and address, the period to be covered, the *inclusion* or *deletion of the Sunday issue* (in the case of *The New York Times*, the library media center may order the Sunday issue *only*) the cost, and if a renewal subscription, so state. A price is usually offered for the nine- or ten-month period. Billing will go to and through the school district business office, in most cases, or direct to the media center, whichever system is adopted by the district. Address and person to whom the paper is to be mailed is essential.

Pamphlets

Pamphlets and any vertical file materials are ordered individually from the publisher with a copy of the order retained by the media specialist, just as is the case with orders for books.

Title						Frequency				
						No. Copies				
	Year		Vol. No.			Year		Vol. No.		
Week Rec'd	1st	2nd	3rd	4th	5th	1st	2nd	3rd	4th	5th
January										
February										
March										
April										
May										
June										
July										
August										
September										
October										
November										
December										

Title													Due
Year	Vol.	Jan.	Feb.	Mar.	Apr.	May	June	July	Aug.	Sept.	Oct.	Nov.,	Dec.

No. Copies   Location   Indexed in

Figure 3.

Since the price is usually nominal, it is better to send money (in the form of a check or money order) with the order, when acceptable to the publisher and possible within the school. Binders are often used for copies which are cataloged into the collection of the center. Others may be filed in the vertical file.

Microfilm or Microfiche

The catalog which lists the largest collection of periodicals, documents, newspapers, and other serial literature available anywhere is that of <u>University Microfilms, 300 North Zeeb Road, Ann Arbor, Michigan 48106.</u> Serials are valuable to the library media center collection. Ordering is simple and can be done on a standing-order basis. This is most satisfactory but does depend upon the budget. The media specialist considering the addition of microfilm and microfilm reader (or fiche) should obtain the latest catalog of available materials and select carefully. The area representative should be contacted as well, for demonstration and discussion of purchase procedures. The catalog is the only verification needed. 3M Company does publish a shorter list of periodicals. The form or format of the film must be decided upon, whether 35mm or 16mm, whether in negative or positive form. The 16mm negative is recommended.

Some considerations are necessary in ordering. If you order microfilm with no index, you cannot exchange it or later add the index to your collection of microfilm. The price is the same for the indexed microfilm and for the unindexed microfilm. The company produces microfilm to order from master microfilm in their collection. It does take six or eight weeks to ship the order to the library media center. On the order you must specify:

> catalog number (from the company catalog)
> title
> inclusive volumes or years for current periodicals
> index or no index (if applicable)
> negative or positive microfilm
> 35mm, microfilm, 16mm, microfilm, or microfiche

type of cartridge, if desired (Kodak and 3M cartridges, add $2.00 for cartridge cost)
complete billing address and, if different, the shipping address

Microfilm is not meant to supplant a subscription to the publisher's paper copies. Libraries entering orders for current periodicals must certify that the library subscribes to the paper edition except as noted below:

1. Out-of-copyright periodicals
2. Not copyrighted, or
3. U.S. government publications

Microfilm is recommended in the library media center in the school, rather than microfiche. A later section of this book discusses the pros and cons of microfilm and microfiche in the library media center.

The media specialist in the school must understand and be able to supervise the techniques related to acquiring materials to support the educational program of the school. Of equal importance are the techniques of making all materials available as efficiently as possible. Management of all these processes are a primary aspect of the school library media specialist's work. Carelessly managed, these record-keeping business and organization procedures can undermine the most creative program of teaching and working with teachers; efficiently managed so as to be almost invisible, they facilitate the program aspects of the media center's work and make it successful.

Notes

1. Gertrude Wulfekoetter. *Acquisition Work: Processes Involved in Building Library Collections.* (Seattle: University of Washington Press, 1961), p. 3.
2. American Library Association. Committee on Library Terminology. A.L.A. *Glossary of Library Terms, with a Selection of Terms in Related Fields,* edited by Elizabeth H. Thompson. (Chicago: American Library Association, 1943), p. 2.

3. Ibid., p. 106.
4. Ibid., p. 37.

For Further Reading

Bloomberg, Marty. *Introduction to Technical Services for Library Technicians*. Littleton, Colo.: Libraries Unlimited, 1971.

Corbin, John B. *A Technical Services Manual for Small Libraries*. Metuchen, N.J.: Scarecrow Press, 1971.

Gillespie, John T. and Spirt, Diana L. *Creating a School Media Program*. New York: Bowker, 1973.

Hensel, Evelyn and Veillette, Peter. *Purchasing Library Materials in Public and School Libraries*. Chicago: American Library Association, 1969.

Marshall, Faye Dix. *Managing the Modern School Library*. West Nyack, N.Y.: Parker Publishing Co., 1976.

Scott, Marian H. *Periodicals for School Libraries: A Guide to Magazines, Newspapers and Periodicals Indexes*. rev. ed. Chicago: American Library Association, 1973.

Taggart, Dorothy T. *A Guide to Sources in Educational Media and Technology*. Metuchen, N.J.: Scarecrow Press, 1975.

VII

Classification and Cataloging in the Library Media Center

Cataloging is "the process of preparing a catalog, or entries for a catalog. In the broad sense, all the processes connected with the preparation and maintaining of a catalog, including classification and assignment of subject headings. In a narrower sense, the determining of the forms of entry and preparing the bibliographical descriptions for a catalog."[1]

A number is assigned to a book or other item, from either the Dewey Decimal System or from the Library of Congress system, and called accordingly either the Dewey Decimal number or the LC number. Books and other media on the same subject may be shelved together in the library media center, but in any case the catalog cards for them will be interfiled, so that anyone searching for material on a subject may find in one place all that is available in all formats—print and nonprint.

Broad classification is the grouping of books in classes or divisions without recognizing the more minute subdivisions. *Close classification* is an arrangement of subjects in detailed subdivisions under a class or division. *Division of a subject:* Subjects or topics subordinate to a class. For example, the graduation in classification may be expressed as follows:

Class—History
Division—North America
Section—United States

Subsections—Civil War
(followed by any degree required)[2]

The classification of materials in the library media center is "the assignment of books and other materials to their proper places in a system of classification."[3]

Since in this chapter we are discussing the problems and solutions for the library media center in the school, we will use the Dewey Decimal system which is most often used in the school or community college library. The bibliography at the end of this chapter gives some additional sources of information for the media specialist who decides to use the Library of Congress system of classification. This may be the case in the larger high school or community college library.

Two prime functions of a classification system are:

1. To serve as a device to group and maintain materials in a logical order on the shelves;
2. To serve as an aid to identify and locate these materials on the shelves.[4]

The Dewey Decimal Classification divides all knowledge into ten main groups:

000 Generalities
100 Philosophy and related disciplines
200 Religion
300 The social sciences
400 Language
500 Pure sciences
600 Technology (Applied sciences)
700 The arts
800 Literature (Belles-lettres)
900 General geography & history[5]

Each of these ten main groups "classify" knowledge into further divisions, the ten additional more specific subject groups. For example, in just this way the 800's are divided:

800 Literature (Belles-lettres)
810 American literature in English
820 English & Anglo-Saxon literatures
830 Literatures of Germanic languages
840 French, Provencal, Catalan
850 Italian, Romanian, Rhaeto-Romanic
860 Spanish & Portuguese literatures
870 Italic languages literatures Latin
880 Hellenic languages literatures
890 Literatures of other languages

Author Letter and Call Numbers

In the Dewey Decimal Classification system all titles on the same subject will have the same number. To provide a unique call number for each book is more important as the collection grows in order to shelve books in some kind of order. Some library media centers use the first one, two, or three letters of the author's name under the classification number. A better method is to use a "book number" in conjunction with the classification number. A book number is "a combination of letters and figures used to arrange books in the same classification number in alphabetical order."[6]

A copy of C. A. Cutter's *Cutter-Sanborn Three-Figure Author Table* (or the Cutter two-figure tables, the Cutter three-figure tables may be used instead of the *Three-Figure Author Table*) is necessary to the library media specialist's collection of professional sources. Follow the directions closely which are a part of the *Tables.*

1) Letter this number on the lower part of the spine, as well as a part of the call number of the book.

2) This number is in three parts: the first part of the author's surname, a series of numbers that represent the remainder of the author's surname, and a "work mark" to distinguish different titles by the same author with the same classification number.

3) It is desirable even in small libraries to use three figures except in certain letters as e, i, o, u, or where the three-figure table uses only two figures.

4) In arrangement on the shelf the figures of the book number are to be considered as decimals and arranged on the shelf in that order.

Juvenile or Books for Young Adults

The addition of the letter J or Y or YA above the Dewey and Cutter numbers will group together books which may be of the category for the younger reader or for the young adult or teenager. However, in the school library media center most of the collection is for the young adult. An E can be used for an easy-read collection. These symbols may be used but in the library media center on the secondary level it is not a recommended practice. Students need to choose books of their own interest level without such symbols to guide them. They should seek books which are of their reading level, guided by the library media specialist; they should not seek out books which will be easy and quick.

A Brief Outline of the Abridged Dewey Decimal System (10th Abridged Edition)

The first edition of the Dewey Decimal System (Decimal Classification) was devised by Melvil Dewey while still a student at Amherst College and was published in 1876. The first abridged edition was published in 1894. Over the years, the abridged and full edition have become closer in concept and coverage. The present Abridged Edition 10 follows the three-volume Edition 18, on which it is based.

The purpose of the Abridged Edition is to provide a short form of classification for the smaller but growing library. The present Abridged Edition is designed primarily for small general libraries, particularly elementary and secondary school and small public libraries, libraries with up to 20,000 volumes and *libraries that do not expect to grow much larger.*[7]

The library media specialist should have at hand the latest edition of the *Abridged Dewey Decimal Classification and Relative Index, Edition 10,* and should know how to use it. In the Introduction of the 10th Abridged Edition there are complete and good instructions for use of the Abridged Edition. The Glossary is also most useful.

The scheme of classification is that each number stands for a subject. All books on the same subject have the same classification number and are shelved together. (See *Second Summary, the 100 Divisons.*)

Fiction. Arrange books alphabetically by author's last name. The symbol F is used in order to arrange all Fiction books together. The author's name can be symbolized by the first three letters of the last name as:

F

Smi (Smith)

This call number arranges a smaller collection quite satisfactorily and also distinguishes the Fiction books as they are separated ready for shelving in the library media center, alphabetically by author. Only the first letter of the author's last name might be used, but the first three letters of the last name are recommended.

Short-Story Collections. A recommended designation for story collections is *SC*, followed by either the last three letters of the author's last name as:

SC

Smi (Smith)

or, the designation SC followed by the Cutter number or book number, which is explained later in this chapter, as:

SC   SS (Story   Collections   or
S643d   Short   Stories)   may   be
           used

For Fiction or Story Collections these are alternatives to the Dewey or Library of Congress classification and are recommended for the library media center in the school as well as for the smaller or medium-sized public library.

Biographies or Autobiographies. The librarian of the library media center should refer to the section *920, Biography, Genealogy, Insignia* of the Abridged Dewey Decimal Classification for specific information.[8] In actual usage in most library media centers the "B" for "biography," *921*, or *92* are used. For biographies of more than one person (collective biography) the number *920* is used, in most cases. A decision must be made and adhered to in regard to classification of biographies. One may elect to class both individual and collected biography of persons associated with a specific subject with the subject. (See the *Abridged Dewey Decimal Classification*, Edition 10, section *920*.)[9]

Reference Books. The letter *R* or *Ref* is often used in the library media center to distinguish materials such as dictionaries, encyclopedias, handbooks, almanacs, or general reference sources which are shelved together in a section as a *reference section* or *area* of the library. Following the *R*, the Dewey Classification and Cutter numbers are used:

R
353
S643d

It is best to group together all reference books designated as such, whether the policy of the library media center is to check them out or not. Having them in a "reference area" brings together students and books, students who are seriously using reference books for research and study and reference sources which are needed.

Use of the Sears List of Subject Headings (10th Edition, Westby)[10]

A *Sears List of Subject Headings* is indispensible to the specialist of the library media center. The present edition, as well as the one previous to this 10th Edition, do not list classification numbers for entries. Dewey Decimal numbers were dropped with the 9th edition. It was considered inconsistent by the publishers to include classification numbers and at the same time instruct the cataloger to consult the Dewey Decimal Classification for numbers. Often the publication was misused when a librarian did not understand the relationship between the subject headings and classification. It was never practical to list all possible Dewey numbers for a particular subject; today it is impossible with the interdisciplinary relationships of subjects and the complexity of assigning subject headings. The library media specialist beginning work in the library media center should read carefully the Introduction entitled: *Subject Headings: Principles and Applications of the Sears List*, as well as the *Directions for Use*.

In addition, it is important to follow the directions in *Sears* on Checking Headings and References in the List and Adding Headings to it. This usage makes your copy of Sears a complete and implicit record of all entries used in your card catalog.

References in the Catalog

References are an important part of the card catalog of the library media center. The reader must be directed to the book that he wants by means of reference to the proper heading.

"See" references. These refer the reader from terms or phrases *not* used as subject headings to terms or phrases that *are* used. They are essential. The reader is directed from variant spellings and terminology to the one word or phrase that has been selected to be used in the catalog. Make "See" references only for those entries which are to be used in the catalog.[11]

"See also" references. "See also" references are concerned entirely with guiding the reader from headings under which he has found books listed to other headings which list books on related or more specific aspects of the subject."[12] This may also be used to guide the reader from words he may think of in using the catalog to those actually used as subject headings. Ordinarily they direct from the *general* subject to a more specific subject, and not, as a rule, from the specific to the general. They are more difficult to make and to understand. Knowledge of the library media center's collection will determine whether "See also" references listed in the *Sears List of Subject Headings* should be used. Many may not be applicable to the small or medium-sized collection.

General references. These are blanket references, either "See" or "See also" which refer to all headings of a particular class. They give the cataloger directions for supplying specific headings omitted from the *List*. They save time and space in the catalog. The library media center specialist should refer to the section in Sears on *General Reference* when cataloging.[13]

Cataloging of Materials in the Library Media Center

Simplified descriptive cataloging is needed in the small to medium-sized library media center. To enter is to record in a catalog a book, a record, a filmstrip set, a tape, or whatever medium it may be. Good sources for simplified descriptive cataloging recommended for the specialist in the library media center are listed at the end of the chapter.

The card catalog is the most widely used form for the catalog of the library media center. Since its function is to record each work in a library by author, translator, editor, illustrator, commentator, series, or by any other person, body, or name under which a reader might look, and to arrange such entries in such a way that all of the works of one author will be found together under the same name, a coordinated procedure must be established. A further purpose of the catalog is to record each work, or even parts of a work, found in the media center under the subjects it treats and to arrange subject entries so that like topics will fall together. A catalog records titles of works and describes each work by giving imprint, title, collation, and notes when necessary. The catalog gives the call numbers by which materials may be located, and the cross references guide a reader from one entry to the other in the catalog.

A catalog's most important function is to meet the needs of the user(s). It must be flexible in terms of making the addition of new materials convenient, and be maintained so as to be up to date. The entire catalog should be physically accessible within the library media center and should enable the user easily to withdraw and replace entries. A card catalog most nearly meets the qualifications for an excellent catalog in the library media center. Listings of new materials or materials placed on reserve can be distributed through the school bulletins.

Author. The author entry is basic and is called the *main entry,* with the author's last name first. It goes on the first line of the main-entry card. The *title* is used first with *nonprint* materials.

Title. Next on the card is the title, with the edition noted. The title is usually entered just as it is on the title page of the book, but in the case of a translation the translation may follow the title or be added as a note; a subtitle may be added.

Imprint. The place, the publisher, and the date of publication, usually found on the title page, are called the *imprint.* The copyright date is often found on the back of the title page. In simplified cataloging the place of publication is often omitted on the catalog card.

Collation. Not on the title page, the collation consists of the *number of volumes,* number of pages, and mentions illustrations, plates, maps, and other illustrative material making up the book.

Notes. Descriptive notes which tell more fully about a book are often used on printed cards, but omitted when cataloging is done in the library media center. In some cases, the catalog will, in addition, contain this information:

> call number—or location device in case of filed materials
> Library of Congress call number
> Library of Congress order number
> Tracing—a list of headings for which additional cards are entered.

Tracing. A tracing is the listing on the card of all the other entries in the card catalog for a particular book or nonbook title. It is used as a record of all entries for a book, the media specialist's record of entries for the particular title used, for example, when the library wishes to withdraw all cards. The tracing contains subject headings numbered consecutively with Arabic numbers. Tracings for other added entries are numbered with Roman numerals (joint author, illustrator, editor, etc.) and follow the subject entries listed. When printed cards are used the tracing is found on all cards, and the usual practice is to place the tracing at the bottom of the main-entry (author) card in cataloging in the library media center.

Unit Card. A unit card is one which can serve as the author card and when duplicated can also serve as the "unit" for all others cards in the catalog, as subject, title, or added entry. All printed cards are considered unit cards, and came into use with the availability of the Library of Congress cards. On hand-written or typed cards still in use, the information is much more brief and, in general, followed the library's particular form. Today the unit cards of the Library of Congress are widely used for all entries in the catalog for a particular book, except perhaps in the case of the series entry. This use of the LC unit card has revolutionized cataloging in most libraries. The expert service of the Library of Congress is available to every library. Each entry of the catalog contains all necessary information. It is standard, less expensive, accurate, and ready for duplication. The MARC II format available to large university libraries is not practical for the school library media center.

For the library which does not utilize unit cards from either the Library of Congress, the H. W. Wilson Company, or one of the book jobbers who provide printed cards, the LC card serves as a model for cataloging in the individual library media center. One card can be ordered and copied. It is the best, most economical, and convenient; the unit cards makes duplication easier. For the neat, attractive, and efficient catalog, it is necessary to use a unit card of some kind. But the *use* of the catalog is the most important thing: does the catalog card really provide the information that is needed by the user of the library media center?

Dictionary Catalog

There are many types of catalogs in use in libraries but in the school library media center the dictionary catalog is the recommended type. An auxiliary catalog which may or may not duplicate the main catalog can be useful. The dictionary catalog is an alphabetical author, title, and subject catalog together with the cross references needed to make the catalog a most useful one. It is helpful for the professional library, for example, to maintain a catalog which catalogs at the minimum all materials available in the professional library for teachers (see Chapter 11). Duplicate cataloging of these professional materials in the main catalog is recommended, thus making all professional materials available also to students. All special collections in fact should be cataloged, either as a part of the main catalog or separately, to insure that all materials in the building, wherever located, are available to all.

Catalog Rules

Rules for cataloging materials in the library media center are not detailed in this chapter, since there is a wealth of books on the subject, some of which the media specialist should have at hand and be able to use. Cataloging is basic to the organization and the utilization program of the library media center.
Some titles include:

> *Anglo-American Cataloging Rules,* North American Text. American Library Association, 1970.

>> Note: This work represents 38 years of work in the codification of cataloging rules for British and American libraries. These rules were drawn up primarily for the general research library, as were all earlier rules of the American Library Association. They are as comprehensive as they could be made to serve the research library.

>> The general acceptance of Library of Congress cards makes it desirable for the smaller library media center to use this code. One code must be adopted for the catalog, to be annotated when any changes or exceptions are made.

> *Commonsense Cataloging:* a Manual for the Organization of Books and Other Materials in School and Small Public Libraries, by Esther J. Piercy. New York, Wilson, 1965.

>> This is a manual for the beginning cataloger and is

an excellent sourcebook for the small library media center. It emphasizes the value of standardization.

Nonbook Materials: the Organization of Integrated Collections, by Jean Riddle Weihs, Shirley Lewis, and Janet Macdonald, in consultation with the CLA, ALA, AECT, EMAC and CAML Advisory Committee on the Cataloging of Nonbook Materials. Ottawa, Canadian Library Association, 1973. (151 Sparks Street, Ottawa, Ontario, Canada KIP 5E3)

> This manual deals with the cataloging of all media and provides for the integration of all materials into a single, unified list of holdings. The cataloging principles are compatible with Parts I and II of the *Anglo-American Cataloging Rules*.

Simple Library Cataloging, by Susan Grey Akers. 5th edition. Scarecrow Press, 1969. (52 Liberty Street, Box 656, Metuchen, N.J. 08840)

> Written for the library worker who lacks professional education and/or experience and for whom implicit directions for accessioning, classifying, and cataloging a collection of printed materials are given. It is a useful book.

Standards for Cataloging Nonprint Material, 3rd edition. Association of Educational Communications and Technology, Information Science Committee. Washington, D.C., AECT, 1972. (1201 Sixteenth Street, N.W., Washington, D.C. 20036)

> The third edition of a practical approach to cataloging of all media.

As the basic key to the library media center's resources, the catalog must provide bibliographic data and descriptions for all items in the collection. Since the locating of nonbook and nonprint materials is done primarily by subject approach, a file

that integrates subject cards for all library holdings might be
the solution for cataloging these items.

Magazines in the Library Media Center

Magazines are organized as simply as possible. When each issue arrives it is stamped with the ownership stamp and acces-
sioned in the file where a card is maintained for each periodical received. The date of issue is checked on the card and the
magazine is then ready for the shelves. Plastic folders are recommended for magazines and journals in the school library
media center both to protect the magazine and to make it more
difficult for a student to take it along. Most school library centers maintain a file of back issues of periodicals dating back
several years, but many titles may be retained indefinitely on
microfilm. Microfilm provides an efficient way to store, maintain, and use valuable back issues in the periodical collection.
Records for all filed magazines should be open and available to
students and faculty.

A *visible periodical record unit* is an efficient way to maintain
the record of all magazines for public use. It records every issue of the magazine the center has, listed by years and months.
Missing copies can be identified, publication frequencies noted,
latest issues noted, as well as other data relative to the title. If
such a visible record is not to be maintained, the library should
at least have a list of periodicals the center has available. This
list should be located near the *Readers' Guide to Periodical Literature* and be available also at the the charge desk. Daily, weekly,
and monthly publications are checked with order cards to record all information pertinent to ordering, renewal, and
pricing.

Periodicals on microfilm should be entered in the visible record
for the user's information. In addition, it is well to maintain a
listing of all periodicals on microfilm near the microfilm reader
and where the film is stored. This may be in the form of a card
file, depending upon the number of titles in microfilm. In the
smaller library media center a list of titles with dates of available periodicals is sufficient.

Checking Out Periodicals. In the secondary library media center particularly where there is much use of back issues of periodicals for research and reference, a *magazine request form* is a great aid. This form is completed by the student whether requesting magazines for use in the library media center or for overnight or longer use. A short-term, check-out period, with the periodical considered a reserve material, is recommended. The form should have space for the name of the student, the class for which research is being done (name of teacher), the date of request, and the full information as given for the title in the *Readers' Guide to Periodical Literature.* It is important for the library media staff to have the full information for locating the magazine, and for the student to have information for finding the reference he needs in the periodical once it is in his hands. For charging, either a magazine charging card or an *overnight book slip* may be used, the latter perfectly satisfactory in the case of periodicals which are to be returned the next day. In many centers the periodical copies which are maintained (perhaps for a five-year period), are considered overnight reserve materials. The student fills out the check-out card, giving title of magazine, date of magazine and with his signature. All overnight check-outs are in a file at the charging desk.

For the larger library media center at least one microfilm reader should be available. *Media Programs: District and State,* (American Library Association and Association for Educational Communications and Technology, 1975,) recommends, as basic for a school of 500 students, availability of two readers, one of which is portable, plus one reader-printer.[14] The reader-printer is an excellent but more expensive addition to the library media center collection. Microfilm are organized in a file cabinet with a card file or listing of film available. *University Microfilms*[15] has the largest and most comprehensive selection of periodicals, documents, newspapers, and other serial literature available on microfilm. It includes thousands of titles dating from as early as 1669 to serials published in the last year. Some library media specialists may still consider the microfilm collection to be an unnecessary expense but it has proved itself to be of value, both in terms of money and in space for storage in the library. Cost is generally less than that of binding, less than reprints or lithographed copies and it serves the same purposes for study and research. Microforms are much easier to maintain in the school library media center and are always available. A collection of periodicals on microfilm which includes titles most used will prove itself of real value in the school library media center.

Shelf List

Among the important organizational records in the library media center, the shelf list is most important. "A Shelf List is a record of the books in a library arranged in the order in which they stand on the shelves."[16] The card for each item contains full bibliographic information, a call number, the number of copies with accession number of each (if such is used), and the price, unless a separate accession record is maintained in which the price is noted. An additional file for nonbook materials when these materials are housed separately is useful, but the entry for nonbook materials should be a part of the shelf-list file. An "equipment" file, in addition, should be maintained. This should include information about vendor, cost, model number, warranty, date of purchase, and a record of repairs.

To the beginning media specialist it may appear that there are an overwhelming number of records to be kept in the media center. There are, but each serves a need and all are helpful in the management of the media center and program. Procedures are more efficient and take less time when there is good organization of the collection. A library media center with fully established procedures operates much more smoothly and efficiently than one in which every problem is a "new" one with no precedent established to provide an answer. You must develop procedures to fit your situation and problems, but some suggested records and procedures which are useful in the library media center are:

shelf list of materials and equipment (first priority)
card catalog (with duplicate cataloging of special collection, as professional library)

quantitative record of current holdings (as book form)
inventory records (from periodic inventories)
subject authority file (may be maintained in *Sears*)[17]
order request file
record of gifts, loans, special collection
periodical holding file (including microfilm)
repair and service file (equipment included, binding)
duplicate catalogs where needed in building or district
handbook for the library media center (philosophy, pro-
    gram, rules, routines)
manual for student assistants in center
manual for instruction in use of the center (teaching)
poster file for displays, idea file

The collection of the library media center will include some materials which do not warrant cataloging. These ephemeral materials should be stored in file folders and arranged alphabetically by subject. A subject list or file should be available which lists and organizes these holdings. A *Sears* subject list is recommended so as to conform with other subject listings in the center. Cards directing the user to this collection should be in the card catalog, as *vertical file, picture file, map file,* etc.

Some years ago many library media centers adopted a color-coded method of cataloging nonbook materials. While this is still an easily used method for some smaller collections where the collection has expanded as the number of types of media has grown, the number of distinctive colors has grown so large that this is no longer a recommended practice. The commercial producers who supply cards for the catalog no longer use the color-coded cards. The recommended method to identify the type of medium within the card catalog, as well as the shelf list, is to use the symbol means of identifying filmstrip, record, sound filmstrip, etc. (FS, RE, SFS, etc.), using this symbol above the call number. The plain catalog card is used, not color banded or in different colors. If the media specialist would like to adapt the color-coded system, the Michigan Association of School Librarians has a useful publication. It is *Cataloging Manual for Nonbook Materials in Learning Centers and School Libraries* and is available from The Bureau of School Services, The University of Michigan, Ann Arbor, Michigan.

The abbreviations for type of nonbook material used in the library media center may be adapted from the *Cataloging Manual for Nonbook Materials in Learning Centers and School Libraries*.[18] These are:

Medium	*Symbol*
charts	C
equipment	EQ
films (8 and 16mm)	F
filmstrips	FS
flashcards	FC
games	GA
globes	G
kits	K
maps	M
models	MO
pictures (posters)	PI
recordings	RE
record albums	RA
slides	SL
specimens	SP
study prints	ST
(transparencies)	
tape recordings	TR

In addition, an entry for *cassette tape recordings* in the card catalog may be *CTR.* The media specialist will find it necessary to devise symbols for other materials which may be in addition to the above list.

Notes

1. American Library Association. Committee on Library Technology, *A.L.A. Glossary of Library Terms, with a Section of Terms in Related Fields*, edited by Elizabeth H. Thompson. (Chicago, American Library Association, 1943), p. 24.
2. Mann, Margaret. *Introduction to Cataloging and Classification of Books*. (Chicago: American Library Association, 1943), p. 36.
3. American Library Association. *Glossary of Library Terms*, p. 30.

4. Corbin, John B. *A Technical Services Manual for Small Libraries.* (Metuchen, N.J.: Scarecrow Press, 1971), p. 100.
5. Dewey, Melvil. *Abridged Dewey Decimal Classification and Relative Index:* devised by Melvil Dewey, Edition 10. (Lake Placid Club, N.Y., Forest Press, 1971), p. 8.
6. American Library Association. *Glossary of Library Terms*, p. 16.
7. Ibid., p. 1.
8. Ibid., p. 88.
9. Ibid., p. 329.
10. Westby, Barbara M., ed. *Sears List of Subject Headings*. 10th ed. (New York: H. W. Wilson, 1972), p. XV.
11. Ibid., p. xv.
12. Ibid., p. xxxii.
13. Ibid., p. 24.
14. American Library Association, and Association for Educational Communications and Technology. *Media Programs: District and School.* (Chicago: American Library Association, 1975). p. 72.
15. University Microfilms, A Xerox Education Company, 300 North Zeeb Road, Ann Arbor, Michigan 48106.
16. American Library Association. *Glossary of Library Terms*, p. 126.
17. Westby, Barbara M., ed. *Sears List of Subject Headings.*
18. Westhuis, Judith Loveys, and others. *Cataloging Manual for Nonbook Materials in Learning Centers and School Libraries.* Michigan Association of School Librarians, 1966.

For Further Reading

American Library Association, and Association for Educational Communications and Technology. *Media Programs: District and School.* Chicago: American Library Association, 1975).

Brown, James W., and Norberg, Kenneth. *Administering Educational Media.* New York: McGraw-Hill, 1973.

Case, Robert N. "Criteria of Excellence: The School Library Manpower Project Identifies Outstanding School Library Centers." *ALA Bulletin*, February 1969, pp. 247–248.

Darling, Richard L. *Streamlining for Service.* (School Activities and the Library, 1965). Chicago: American Library Association, 1965.

Darling, Richard L. "The Library's Becoming the Focal Place." *Instructor* 77 (November 1967): 90–91.

Ellsworth, Ralph. *The School Library.* New York: Center for Applied Research in Education, 1965.

Erickson, Carleton W. H. *Administering Instructional Media Programs.* New York: Macmillan, 1968.

Fader, Daniel, and McNeil, Elton B. *Hooked on Books: Program and Proof.* New York: Putnam, 1968.

Fargo, Lucille. *The Library in the School.* Chicago: American Library Association, 1947.

Galvin, Thomas J. *Problems in Reference Service: Case Studies in Method and Policy.* New York: Bowker, 1965.

Gaver, Mary V. *Services of the Secondary School Media Centers: Evaluation and Development.* Chicago: American Library Association, 1971.

Hickey, Doralyn J. *Problems in Organizing Library Collections.* New York: Bowker, 1972.

"Libraries in Secondary Schools, A New Look." *Bulletin of the National Association of Secondary School Principals,* January 1966, p. 122.

Lohrer, Alice, ed. *The School Library Materials Center: Its Resources and Their Utilization.* Champaign, Ill.: The Illini Union Bookstore, 1964.

Nickel, Mildred L. *Steps to Service: A Handbook of Procedures for the School Library Media Center.* Chicago: American Library Association, 1975.

Pearson, N. P., and Butler, Lucius. *Instructional Materials Centers: Selected Readings.* Minneapolis: Burgess, 1969.

Prostano, Emanuel T., and Prostano, Joyce C. *The School Library Media Center.* Littleton, Colo.: Libraries Unlimited, 1971.

Purdy, Robert, and Finch, Arnold. "Getting the Most out of In-Service Education." *Teachers' Encyclopedia.* Englewood Cliffs, N.J., Prentice-Hall, 1966, p. 907.

Rufsvold, Margaret. *Audio-Visual School Library Service.* Chicago: American Library Association, 1959.

Silber, Kenneth, "What Field Are We In, Anyhow?" *Audiovisual Instruction,* May 1970, p. 22.

Silberman, Charles E. "High Schools that Work: Murder in the Classroom," part 3. *The Atlantic* 226 (August 1970): 87.

Stone, C. Walter. "Library Uses of the New Media of Commu-
    nication," edited by C. Walter Stone. *Library Trends,* Oc-
    tober 1967, p. 120.
*Student Use of Libraries: An Inquiry into the Needs of Students, Li-
    braries, and the Educational Process.* Papers of the Confer-
    ence within a Conference. Chicago: American Library As-
    sociation, 1964.
*Study of Circulation Control Systems: Public Libraries, College and
    University Libraries, Special Libraries.* LTP Publication no. 1.
    George Fry and Associates, Inc. Chicago: American Li-
    brary Association, 1961.
Swanker, Esther. "Maximum Use of the Library." *American
    School Board Journal* 151 (November 1965): 32–33.

VIII
Use of the Library
Media Center

Circulation Procedures

Accessibility of materials to the users of the school library media center is the reason for any circulation system. Control systems are necessary but they exist *to make materials accessible* so that the user can find what he wants, have it available, and use it as he needs to. It is important to both students and teachers that there be easy access to materials, that there be as few as possible areas of contention or friction, and that the system be cost effective. Whatever system is devised should be simple and yet comprehensive enough to provide statistics as they are needed. Most school library media centers are not large enough to be able to afford mechanical, photographic or electronic devices, although there are many in use in school media centers today. Such systems require identification cards or plates, and to maintain these and have them available, it is usually advisable for the library to file them in the school. Otherwise, they may be lost.

In general, the user of the library media center in the school forms his opinion of the services of the center on the basis of the services at the circulation or charge desk. The procedures should be simple and pleasant from the user's point of view.

The essential elements of a practical circulation system are a book card and date-due slip. A system known as the Newark

(New Jersey) Circulation System is used in most media centers
over the country. Its operation is very simple and can be handled by clerical or student library assistants. The user signs his
name and the date due is stamped on the same line and immediately following the signature. The book cards are then
filed under due date by call number or alphabetically by author. To renew materials for further use the same procedure
is used or duplicated. It is important that both the book card
(or material card in the case of nonbook materials or equipment) is stamped with the same date as that which appears on
the date-due slip in the book.

The same basic system used for books is recommended for
the circulation of nonbook materials and for periodicals as
well. A book card should be available for all media in circulation from the media center. On some materials and equipment
it is impossible to attach a book pocket; a blank book card may
be so noted and used for such materials, filed under *equipment*
or *audiovisual materials* at the charge desk. Some media centers
use printed *overnight cards* for such materials or for periodicals.
Overnight checking of vertical file materials is usually satisfactory for adequate use.

Reserve materials, whether curricular or student request reserves, must be handled systematically. A *reserve slip* is usually
used although sometimes a request form or a list of requested
reserve materials is maintained. The cards for materials
checked out to teachers are usually filed in a separate charging
tray; the material may represent a classroom collection which
is to be retained throughout the school year. This requires a
separate guide card for each teacher. A flagging device in the
circulation file can be used—a paperclip on a bookcard of a
book requested for reserve, or a transparent book card cover.
When the item is returned, the circulation clerk is alerted to
hold the material as requested.

Liberal borrowing periods are important to make materials
accessible; however, in cases in which materials are in heavy
demand it is necessary to have shorter periods of use for maximum accessibility. If the center has a large collection with duplicate copies, restrictive loan policies are not necessary. In the
case of materials needed for instruction in the classroom, a

long-term loan is recommended, sometimes for the entire
school year or a full semester. In this case, the date of check
out is stamped on the book card or material card. At some
stated times during the year it is necessary to check on faculty
loans to see if materials are no longer in use and can be returned to the center for further access.

A policy of no limit on the number of materials which can be
checked out from the media center by one individual is desirable, but reasonable limits may be necessary. Heavily used reference books may have to be noncirculating, for use in the center only, or loaned on overnight loan only. Media on reserve
by classes or teachers, current periodicals, filed periodicals,
equipment, or in some cases, audiovisual materials, are usually
on overnight reserve. A longer reserve period may be established by faculty request or when practical.

Overdue materials are a real problem with media specialists in
the schools today. The traditional view that fines are useful for
bringing back materials is still widely accepted. Other media
specialists may feel that fines are unnecessary, that they are
negative, do nothing to build responsibility in the individual
student, and are not even an effective deterrent. Collecting
fines is time consuming and can arouse hostility. However, loss
of materials is a real problem in today's media centers; there is
a great deal more loss by theft or destruction than in former
years. A compromise policy might be to place fines on materials needed on day-to-day basis in the center, such materials
as reference sources, audiovisual materials, reserve books, and
periodicals. The decision to levy or not to levy fines is one that
must be made by the individual media center, but whether or
not the media center does so, there must be some means to in-
sist to both students and faculty that they return materials.
Sending overdue notices to students can become a big task; a
list to classes enlisting teacher reinforcement is sometimes effective, while multicopy overdue notices are satisfactory in
most cases. Overdue notices in the case of reserve or much
needed materials must go out as soon as the material is overdue. In the case of materials not immediately needed a regular
weekly schedule for notification will suffice. In cases of real ne-
glect or vandalism it is sometimes necessary to notify the parents of students.

Loss or damage of material is the responsibility of the student who has checked the materials from the center. The media specialist must realize that sometimes accidents are unavoidable and the cost of some losses must be assumed by the center as part of operations. Decisions made by the media staff should be fair and reasonable and acceptable to the administrator.

Consideration of Circulation of Audiovisual Materials

If the media center has a broad collection of books, there may be no need for a limit on the number of books checked out of the center by an individual. However, in the case of audiovisual materials and equipment, where the collection is necessarily limited by cost, it is important to keep all items in circulation and available to all users. Equipment check out is often a problem. It can best be solved by having a check-out card on each piece of equipment, by housing the equipment in a particular area of the media center or professional library, and by strictly limiting the length of time it may be kept, depending on need and how it is being used. A chart or request form may be used to reserve needed equipment, as by a teacher in the classroom. In some media centers a complicated schedule is maintained telling where each piece of equipment is at all hours. On the other hand, to check out each piece of equipment with a check-out card with the understanding that all equipment is returned as soon as it is used is a very satisfactory method. With each piece of equipment numbered and cataloged, the file of checked-out materials is a ready reference for the media specialist as to where each piece of equipment is being used. However, there must be provision for reserves of equipment.

A concern of media specialists is the means of checking out the great variety of media materials. Wherever a book or material card can be attached, this system is recommended. However, in the case of a filmstrip, a tape, a blank videotape or reel-to-reel tape, a cassette, a single record of an album, a transparency, and other materials of this kind, it is better to have a check-out card prepared and available at the charge

desk on which can be written or typed the item name, identification number or accession number, the signature of the person borrowing, and the date due, if so stamped. Different color
cards can be used for identification of materials which are
checked out on forms other than the usual book or charge
card.

Circulation Records

Circulation records are useful, but not the only indicators of
the use to which materials are put outside of the media center.
Which materials are most frequently used? Are they borrowed
in connection with classroom use? Do students on their own
enjoy or seek information in these sources? Do assignments
stimulate use? Circulation records may show that a fine collection of materials in a specific subject area is not being used as
it could be. Such a discovery may point the way to specific in-
service training for teachers to acquaint them with these materials and to identify learning projects that might utilize them.
There may need to be more publicity on materials available to
teachers, as well as to students. A little study of circulation patterns may point out that restrictions are too narrow, and accessibility too limited. The circulation records may help to determine the size of the collection which is needed in particular
subject areas, and show how many items a particular student
borrowed during the school year. It must be remembered,
however, that there is a great increase in use of reference materials in the center which does not show up in circulation
figures.

Hours of Service

The hours during which the library is open are an important
consideration for both students and teachers. Serious thought
should be given to evening hours, Saturday morning hours,
and an extended school day for library media center hours.
The important thing is to serve the needs of the students as

identified through survey and statistical methods as well as by
student request. The library media center, in general, should
be open at least forty minutes before school begins and again
at least that long *after* the close of regularly scheduled classes.
This will vary according to bus schedules, the location of the
school, other after-school activities, and the availability of an
adequate public library system serving students' home communities. Students should not be limited to any significant degree in their use of the library media center or in freedom to
borrow from the center. All of this has an effect on library circulation and must be considered as one reviews the center's
procedures and statistics. Circulation figures can be valuable
only if they are kept accurately.

Expert cataloging is an important factor in making materials
accessible and available. Together with good circulation procedures and records it helps to determine the level of contribution of the media center to the school and its total program.
The well-organized and well-maintained media center that is in
the mainstream of school life will serve the needs of both faculty and students and will be the one place where everyone can
go for information and stimulation, whether the need is related to personal interests or classroom requirements.

Scheduling and Student Use of the Library Media Center

The object of any plan for use of the library media center is
to make its resources easily accessible to users, whether an individual student or faculty member, or a group. Students who
want to use the center should be able to when and as they wish.
In schools with flexible scheduling students have real freedom
of choice in their use of the media center. In others with more
rigid scheduling, classes may come to the center on a scheduled
basis, or even without any advance scheduling. The latter is
possible only if the facility is large enough. A teacher can then
feel free to bring the class, or a part of the class, to the center
as instruction provides need and stimulus. In many schools
now, students have complete freedom of choice as to where
they may spend an hour for which they are not scheduled dur-

ing the school day. During such a period they may go to the media center, they may go home, or downtown, or to a student lounge area. In other schools, students may need a pass from the classroom teacher to come to the media center. This is often the case in the use of released time from the classroom. In some cases, restrictive policies have to be adopted to limit the number of users during any one period to the capacity of the media center, or to keep track of students and to know which ones are in the center at any given hour. The media specialist can learn much by talking with other media center specialists and knowing what policies are effective, what methods work well and, in this way, devise a plan that is thought to be a good one. Each school situation differs, so a "try out" tells the story.

It is helpful to the staff of the media center to know a day or so in advance when an entire class or even small groups will be using the center. There may be reserve materials to make ready; it may be necessary to collect materials for the class to use or to set aside an area so that the class can work together in one section of the center or in a small meeting room. A *sign-up* sheet may be used for this purpose, or arrangements may be made informally with the media specialist. A *sign-in* sheet works very well in order that teachers may know that a group from the classroom has been in the media center and has remained for a given period of time.

There are many ways of publicizing and promoting the media center and its materials with students. They should be encouraged to offer suggestions about both procedures and materials. It should be constantly kept in mind—everybody's mind—that not only student reading, but listening and viewing experiences are all related to the media center. A tape, kept up to date by the students, can tell of the new materials in the center; or a talk-it-over can highlight new books or new ideas students have. Periodic discussion sessions in the center will help the media specialist take advantage of many ideas offered by students for making the center a place to be used and enjoyed.

Students will often make requests for materials to be secured by the media specialist on interlibrary loan, materials for a term paper, or just to find out about something of interest. Students may request that the media center collect books for a special subject, or that the media specialist work with him in organizing materials for a paper or research study.

An occasional special library media center bulletin may be read by students, but a regular column in the school bulletin will be more effective. Variety is important in planning public relations with students. Remember, these are children of change; systems may be effective today but ignored tomorrow. They are children of television and TV advertising techniques; they like posters and visual displays, but even more they like action, something happening to attract their attention. There are many special ways of promoting the media center with students, and the creative media specialist will enlist the ideas of students and their help in carrying them out: bulletin board displays, brief reviews written by students, posters, contests, and special programs.

Orientation Instruction in Library Use

Orientation of students, particularly of the student who is new in the school, is important. Again, it is best to make an occasion. It is well to have an open-house announcement at the beginning of the school year to invite new students to come to the media center. Personal attention and a reason for showing the new student the media center are best. Confer with the teacher, find a reason to bring the new student into the library media center and take time to visit with him, to show him where all materials are, how the library media center is organized, and how the equipment works. Whole classes entering the school for the first time should be provided with several orientation sessions and a clearly written manual.

In surveying the research and the materials prepared in this subject area, one finds that really very little has been written on the subject of library instruction for the student as he first begins to use the library media center. Students, particularly those planning postsecondary education or training of any kind must know how to obtain and use information in the library and should be equipped with the keys to the resources. The library media specialist will be the chief instructor, or failing that the college librarian once the student reaches the col-

lege level, but a sense of need—motivation to learn the lifelong usable search skills—must be stimulated in the student.
He will feel more at home in the media center if he knows how
its collection is organized, where materials are, and how to do
work independently. Independent study is an important use
aspect of the media center and is particularly attractive to students who like to plan their own projects and seek what they
want to know on their own.

Library instruction, or the teaching of the uses of the library
media center, is best approached by relating it to a specific
problem or assignment. A workshop setting is best for instruction in library skills. Even though a student may use only one
or two reference books, he enjoys being competent to discover
what he wants to know. The trend in library instruction is def-
initely away from teaching skills by the reference tool: the use
of the encyclopedia or the dictionary per se, even when such
categorical instruction is organized into study units. Doing it
this way, the student does not see the usefulness of what he is
doing and usually will remember little of it. Very little is known
actually about teaching skills in study. Students want to know,
but they like to have a reason for doing something.

Teaching students how to use the library media center as a
part of a research project term paper or study they are working on is important. Here students see a need for what they are
using and doing. They will remember information and sources
they use to gather their assignment project information. The
specialized library tools as reference sources should not consti-
tute a "library lesson," but be a part of a broader assignment
utilizing these tools—the best instruction on the use of the library and its sources as a means to a particular end.

The best way to accomplish this and meet at the same time
the needs which the teacher sees for study of a specific reference source, is to treat the library media center as a laboratory,
using a workshop approach to reference. This method is also
effective with teachers, as the media specialist seizes upon their
need for reference resources in a particular curriculum area,
and reminds them how to find and use what they need. As the
class (or group of faculty) gathers, the media specialist can
briefly introduce them to sources, the nature of the materials,
and how they are used. The classroom teacher should work

closely with the media specialist and her own students to explain or interpret information. Students should not be inter-
rupted as they begin work; they do best working on their own.
Instruction should come first, then "hands-on" practice.

Whatever scheduling pattern is utilized by a school, the library reference workshop should be included, whether formally or informally. At the time of a research assignment for
a senior class, for instance, the media specialist should be ready
and prepared to introduce them to reference sources they may
not know, to explain the use of specific sources. It is an opportunity for superior teaching on the part of the media specialist.
Ask yourself, "What do I need to know?" Putting yourself in
the place of the student coming to the media center to begin
the research assignment. A summary of reference sources can
be prepared and presented as interestingly as possible using
examples. Some questions may be as these:

> How do I select from among the articles given in *Readers'
> Guide*? Which will be most helpful to me?
> What titles of books do you have on my subject? Which
> would be most useful to me on this assignment?
> How shall I get the information from the book? (This is
> often a problem with students, the abstracting of the
> information needed.)
> What good is the card catalog to me on this subject?
> How do I list this book in my bibliography?

The creative library media specialist who knows the students
and teachers well, and who knows the collection of the media
center and how to use the sources will have no problems in
teaching the skills of library use and research.

For Further Reading

Advanced Library Reference Skills (Transparency) Collaborator:
Mary Ann Swanson. Encyclopaedia Britannica Educational Corp., EB 24947. Chicago: Encyclopaedia Britannica Educational Corp., 1970.

Aldrich, Ella V. *Using Books and Libraries*. 4th ed. Englewood Cliffs, N.J.: Prentice-Hall, 1960.

Busby, Edith. *What Does a Librarian Do?* New York: Dodd, 1963.

Cook, Margaret G. *The New Library Key*. 3rd ed. New York: H. W. Wilson, 1975.

Downs, Robert B. *How to Do Library Research*. Urbana: University of Illinois Press, 1975.

Gates, Jean Kay. *Guide to the Use of Books and Libraries*. 2nd ed. New York: McGraw-Hill, 1969.

Hopkinson, Shirley L. *Instructional Materials for Teaching the Use of the Library: A Selected, Annotated Bibliography of Films, Filmstrips, Books and Pamphlets, Tests and Other Aids*. 4th ed. San Jose: Claremont House, 1971.

Guidance Associates. *The Library: What's In It for You?* New York: Guidance Associates, 1975. (Sound Filmstrip)

Hanna, G. R., and McAllister, M. K. *Books, Young People and Reading Guidance*. 2nd ed. New York: Harper, 1968.

Lohrer, Alice. *The School Library Materials Center: Its Resources and Their Utilization*, edited by Alice Lohrer. Champaign, Ill.: Illinois Union Bookstore, 1964.

Lieberman, Irving. *A Working Bibliography of Commercially Available Audio-visual Materials for the Teaching of Library Science*. Occasional Paper, no. 94. Urbana: University of Illinois Graduate School of Library Science, 1968.

Meetham, Roger. *Information Retrieval*. New York: Doubleday, 1970.

Meyer, Edith Patterson. *Meet the Future: People and Ideas in the Libraries of Today and Tomorrow*. Boston: Little Brown, 1964.

Rossoff, Martin. *Library in High School Teaching*. 2nd ed. New York: H. W. Wilson, 1961.

Rossoff, Martin. *The School Library and Educational Change*. Littleton, Colo.: Libraries Unlimited, 1971.

Santa, Beauel M., and Hardy, Lois Lynn. *How to Use the Library*. Palo Alto: Pacific Books, 1955.

Sayers, Frances Clarke. *Anne Carroll Moore*. New York: Atheneum, 1972.

Toser, Marie A. *Library Manual; A Study-Work Manual of Lessons on the Use of Books and Libraries.* 6th ed. New York: H. W. Wilson, 1964.

3M Company. *Library Science: Dewey Decimal System, English packet No. 9.* (Transparencies) (St. Paul, Minn.: 3M Company, n.d.)

Calendar of the Year's Program

September

Orientation of new faculty during two orientation in-service days before opening of school term.

A workshop approach is suggested for faculty at which specifics can be discussed, production facilities explained, and collections in each teaching area investigated, so that all teachers will know about materials and available equipment, and procedures. A half-day session should be set aside for new teachers only.

Orientation of all students, inviting classes through English or Language Arts classes but not restricted to these classes, scheduled during month.

A workshop approach is much better than a "tour-of-the-library" approach. Students enjoy solving problems and like to feel they are finding their way for themselves. The workshop should be built around a class assignment but giving the student freedom to choose subjects.

A Handbook of the Library Media Center is available for all students and classes and in the center. Any necessary revision of the Handbook completed early in September. Sessions with student librarians reviewing all areas of media center operation, responsibilities.

A Newsletter to faculty on a bi-monthly basis to include many areas of the center, new materials, programs, services.

Classes begin use of the library media center coming with the teacher for group use of the facility. Open-ended, no scheduling, unless it becomes necessary; teachers should feel free to come at any time with the class. A scheduling sheet is at hand if needed; the media center may need to resolve conflicts.

In-service Day for instruction in all equipment. 3–5 in-service days should be planned for in the school year and set up with the administration. Emphasize different areas at each one. Uses of equipment should be the first; new teachers should be invited personally but it is a good opportunity to include teachers who have problems in the operation of equipment. Review of all new audiovisual equipment and materials.

Emphasize *public relations with the student body* by occasional items in the student bulletin, student paper, announcements, or invitations. Do these on a scheduled basis so as to be consistent and constant.

October

Bi-monthly bulletin distributed to teachers. Use attractive format.
Monthly report to Board of Education. See suggested form for report.
Begin *order file* to include all books not received from summer orders. Monthly ordering is recommended, more frequently for larger center.
Where no central processing is available, this is a continuous process.
Make plans for Open House for Education Week; include brochure, exhibits, demonstration, tour.
Request order suggestions for *Title IV, ESEA* orders (tentative approval of orders from district or state offices). Formerly Title II, ESEA.
Conclude student orientation for classes not able to come in September.
Attend any district and area professional meetings.

November

Open House during Education Week: news story, invitations to parents, arrange for student guides, displays.
Orders for Title IV, ESEA completed for approval for spring ordering.
Monthly orders ready to mail, or to central office for processing.
Newsletters to faculty (bi-monthly) to include library center news, new collections, books on reserve, total collection figures; opportunity for communication in many areas.
Monthly report to Board of Education. Include circulation statistics, class and student use figures, total collection, additions to center by type of material. *See suggested form.*
Plan and prepare holiday bulletin boards, supplemented with book displays.
Attend any area or regional or state professional meetings.
In-service day, professional library collection emphasized, use of professional library, services to faculty.

December

Assemble reserve material requests for term paper and research writing.
Newsletter to Faculty. Include an invitation for an open house in professional library (refreshments)
Holiday Open House for faculty.
Christmas get-together for student librarians.
Title applications and other state applications ready and mailed.
Mail any orders early in the month (December particularly).

January

Planned communiques in the student daily bulletin, at least once a week is sug-
gested. Brief, timely, interesting to students.
Bi-monthly bulletin to faculty; *Previews* of media center collection.
Selection sources on display and assembled in the teachers library; forms for or-
der requests at hand.
Reminder on order requests so as to culminate at end of the year, as well as
periodically.
Meeting time set for meetings with other librarians in district; plan this for monthly
meetings, at least several through the year.
Monthly report to the Board of Education. Include any publications as *Previews*
(monthly bulletin to faculty) and proposed budget for coming year.
Monthly orders mailed as ready, verified, and checked.
Reading of all shelves and materials, searching of lost items, semiannual.

February

Attendance at Board of Education meeting, on adoption and changes in district
selection policy, budget.
In-service day with faculty. Emphasize different areas on successive in-service
days. In February, the learning laboratory or operation of equipment within
the center. One of five scheduled in-service days, arranged with the cooperation of the administration for the year's scheduling.
Monthly orders. Begin work on verification and searching of an end-of-the-year
order when new budgeted money is available.
Public relations news story to local newspapers or an area publication. Develop
a contact person with the media. Occasional news stories are worthwhile
and of interest.
Faculty bi-monthly newsletter.
Many classes in the center this month, scheduling may become a necessity.
Regular scheduling of the learning laboratory (electronic) by language, English,
business (shorthand dictation) classes.

March

Checking of all shelves, in sequence, for order, condition, and repair of all
materials.
Overall review of class use of the library media center, discussion with teachers,
arranging for research materials, reserve areas, etc.
Include in newsletter to faculty a request for ordering suggestions, listing of inter-
esting new materials ordered and added.
Regular monthly orders mailed.
Report to Board of Education or principal.
Class use is heavy in March, prearrange with faculty to have materials ready.

April

Plan for end-of-year procedures, discuss with aides and with student assistants
    to schedule all activities, procedures.
Complete verification and search for all end-of-year orders on hand.
Supplies ordered, periodicals; review any display of books for purchase available
    in area, adding to the order file.
Monthly newsletter to faculty; request for evaluation from students and faculty.

May

Complete reading of shelves early in month, continual checking for lost titles.
Orders to business office for mailing, or to district for processing.
Annual report begun, complete at end of month.
Final newsletter to faculty, request suggestions.
Bring visible periodical record up to date.
Cumulative report completed, to include year's circulation, additions to collection,
    number of users, number of classes in center, professional library
    circulation.
Last week of school year media center closed for final searching, completing any
    checking for lost titles, all materials in, survey of all materials.

IX

Records and Maintenance
in the Library Media Center

In this day of emphasis on accountability it is *very important* to maintain accurate and complete records of all kinds for the library media center. They are vital for financial reasons in the preparation of the budget; they are important for evaluative purposes; they are important for professional standing if one is to be considered *reliable* and *responsible,* as the word is defined today. In today's school climate, one often needs to explain reasons, causes, grounds, or motives for doing things in a particular way. Records are important for many reasons but perhaps most of all for self-evaluation and improvement in the media center program. They indicate areas for change or revision of program. They support communications with the board of education, with faculty members or with the administration, and help to make concrete for them the breadth and scope of the library media center program, the visions and plans for the future. Records need to be maintained for several areas of the library media center program: financial, service, organizational, and archival records of the center and of the school.

Financial Records

Depending upon the organization of the business operations of the school district, financial records will be maintained either by the library media center itself or in the business office of the district. A recommendation is that the media specialist retain a copy of all financial transactions in addition to those maintained by the district business office. Such records will include:

> *budget proposals,* to include the annual budget allocated by the district as well as those funded by ESEA, or other title monies.
>
> *budget allocations and accounting,* to include the running account of the library media center with the balance at the beginning of the year, with itemized monthly expenditures. The media specialist should know at any given time the amount of money available in the media center budget allocation.
>
> *petty cash fund,* to include an accounting accurately by each month with individual entries of amounts spent. This may be accomplished through the individual building activities fund where the media specialist has an amount established to take care of smaller items, immediate purchases, etc.
>
> *requisition and purchase orders,* to include duplicates of any requisitions or purchases requested to be made by the business office. A form is usually in use for this purpose, a copy of which is retained. These orders and purchases are approved by the building principal as well, in most cases, the money coming from the budgeted amount set aside for the library media center; requisitions may come from supplies maintained by the school district, but copies of requisitions should be maintained.
>
> *receipt of any gifts, monies, or expenditures* which are outside the budget of the media center or regular financial procedures. These may include gifts from a book club, from an individual, in the form of money or items for the collection. Expenditures may be for leadership training for the student assistants, paraprofessionals in the center, or for telephone calls.

receipts of materials ordered, invoices, the filing of shipping
invoices and the listing of materials which remain on
an order to be received (partial order).

current statement of expenditures, as maintained on a monthly
basis to supplement the accounting in the district
business office. This gives the media specialist an accounting of expenditures by the month, which is
helpful in preparing the annual budget.

Organizational Records

These are familiar to the experienced media specialist, but
for the less experienced they are included here to serve as a
checklist of records that need to be maintained.

Shelf list of all materials and equipment as cataloged in the
library media center. This may include materials on
loan to the classroom on a yearly basis, all equipment in the building, the collection of the professional library as well as the main library media center, all audiovisual materials. This is a classified card
file of all the holdings of a media center, with full
bibliographic information, the number of copies,
cost, and source where an accession record is not
maintained.

Inventory records or accession records when used.

Quantitative record of current holdings (Use a Classified Summary of Additions and Withdrawals record book in
addition to summary statements prepared monthly.)

Records of materials or equipment out for repair, rebinding,
etc.

Periodical holdings. A visible format is best, materials for
which can be ordered from the library supply
houses. This alphabetically arranges the periodicals
with a record of each issue held by the library media
center. Record cards should also be maintained
which list copies as received and note copies not yet

MANAGEMENT AND ADMINISTRATION

received. A listing of periodicals in the library media center should also be prepared for each classroom and for individual availability in the center.

Records of gifts or loans from other libraries or individuals, corporations. If the library media center receives a copy of a periodical or a collection of periodicals from any source as a gift there should be an accurate record. Many communities give items to the school library media center.

On-order records. This may be a card file of materials on order but should be kept up to date and maintained daily.

Material requests. This is a card file usually, which lists the materials faculty or students want or that the media specialist sees a need for. Maintain a listing of addresses for ordering as well.

Subject-authority file. The usual procedure in the library media center is to maintain in the current edition of *Sear's List of Subject Headings* an accurate record of all entries used as subject headings in the catalog of the library media center.

Card catalog, and in some cases a *book catalog.* Where a book catalog is available it should be placed in duplicate in many classrooms. This is desirable but is not possible for financial reasons in many school library media centers. A possibility is the maintenance of a listing of all audiovisual materials available in the community in book catalog form. Card catalog should be complete and up to date at all times to include all materials in the library media center. Careful cataloging is most important.

Service Records

These are records which detail all of the services provided by the library media center insofar as possible. A sign-in record may be maintained to give the number of students using the center daily. A record may be made of all bibliographic searches undertaken; the number of bibliographies prepared; reference questions answered; teacher planning hours; attendance and class use of the library media center. Circulation figures will be carefully kept, but any measures that show the tremendous volume of in-library media center services and use are doubly valuable. Most nonlibrarians—especially those who control pursestrings are inclined to measure library use and effectiveness exclusively in terms of books circulated. Other statistical data do support a budgetary request or expressed need for more clerical, technical, or professional help in the library media center. The decisions about what records to keep will be largely those of the media specialist in the school, with the advice of the principal weighed large! Statistics *can* be overdone, so evaluation must be made as to whether they serve a worthwhile purpose or are just busy work. Certain statistics must of course be kept to meet the requirements of the state department of education, of accrediting agencies, of the federal government where title funding is involved, and of the school district. The media specialist must know what statistics the center will be expected to produce. Forms are available for many of the statistics used from the library supply houses. Records to be kept should include:

> *Job description, library staff,* description of positions available and needed.
> *Circulation records,* usage of all audiovisual equipment and materials as well as books.
> *Attendance records*
> *Classroom use of the library media center* records, include library instruction.
> *Handbook of the Library Media Center* (keep up to date)
> *Procedural Manual* for use with aides, clerical persons, paraprofessional help.

Archival Records

Such records will include a collection of important documents, newspapers, bulletins, and yearbooks of the school and of the media center. News stories and professional publication and community newspaper or PTA newsletter write-ups, which tell of the library media center and its program or leaders, should be on file. Policy statements, administrative announcements, professional organization communications for both the media specialists and for teachers, statistical data organized for the year— anything which will be of value and interest to the administrator, the teachers, or the media center should be maintained. These often can be stored in the professional library where they are available for research and use. These are the written record of the history of the school and of the media center. This collection may be expanded by minutes, reports, programs of events, newspaper clippings of school activities— the list is endless, and is at the discretion of the media specialist and the administrator.

For Further Reading

American Library Association, and Association for Educational Communications and Technology. *Media Programs: District and School.* Chicago: American Library Association, 1975.

Bloomberg, Marty, and Evans, Edward G. *Introduction to Technical Services for Library Technicians.* Littleton, Colo.: Libraries Unlimited, 1971.

Corbin, John B. *A Technical Services Manual for Small Libraries.* Metuchen, N.J.: Scarecrow Press, 1971.

Davies, Ruth Ann. *The School Library: A Force for Educational Excellence.* New York: Bowker, 1973.

Erickson, Carlton W. H. *Administering Instructional Media Programs.* New York: Macmillan, 1968.

Gaver, Mary V. *Services of Secondary School Media Centers: Evaluation and Development.* Chicago: American Library Association, 1971.

Hickey, Doralyn J. *Problems in Organizing Library Collections.* New York: Bowker, 1972.

Nickel, Mildred L. *Steps to Service: A Handbook of Procedures for the School Library Media Center*. Chicago: American Library Association, 1975.

Prostano, Emanuel T. *School Media Programs: Case Studies in Management*. Metuchen, N.J.: Scarecrow Press, 1970.

Prostano, Emanuel T., and Prostano, Joyce S. *The School Library Media Center*. Littleton, Colo.: Libraries Unlimited, 1971.

Rossoff, Martin. *The School Library and Educational Change*. Littleton, Colo.: Libraries Unlimited, 1971.

Saunders, Helen E. *The Modern School Library: Its Administration as a Materials Center*. Metuchen, N.J.: Scarecrow Press, 1968.

Sullivan, Peggy., ed. *Realization: The Final Report of the Knapp School Libraries Project*. Chicago: American Library Association, 1968.

X

The Paperback Collection
in the Library Media Center

In recent years there have been an increasing number of research studies on the use of paperbacks in the school, all pointing to the fact that paperbacks are a vital medium of the day, well suited to the mobile, casual lifestyle of today's student. Perhaps the outstanding research study, and the one most pertinent to the media center in the school, is the 1967 and the 1970 follow-up study of the American Association of School Librarians, the American Book Publishers' Council, and *School Management* magazine, with other cooperating organizations.[1] In the update in 1970 by John T. Gillespie and Diana L. Spirt, the principle change was that responses were made only by librarians, while those in 1967 were from librarians, principals, and other administrators, so the 1970 responses reflect the opinions and data from the library field alone. In 1967 and again in 1970, almost 93 percent of the schools surveyed used paperbacks in one or more ways. Both studies point to the more extensive use of paperbacks in the secondary school than in the elementary school. Other conclusions gained by correlating statistics from the two studies are:

> Urban schools use paperbacks much more than rural schools.
> Schools without libraries use paperbacks much more frequently.

Urban schools outrank rural schools in amount of use per
   title.
The larger the library the greater the use of paperbacks.
Schools that have bookstores incorporate paperbacks into
   their curricular studies with greater frequency than
   those without bookstores.
Overall use has increased with 73% noting an overall rise
   in usage.[2]

At all levels of use, the chief reasons for use are that students
prefer them and that the paperbacks are less expensive than
hardcover format. They are practical for short-term loans;
many titles are available in paperback format that are not available in hardback. Many titles for adult readers are original in
paperback format; juvenile books in paperback are more often
reprints. The least significant motivating factor for use in secondary school media centers is the amount of space required
for housing the paperbacks since this depends upon method of
shelving or housing. Processing costs are not a factor here as
many media specialists do not catalog fully the paperback edition of a book. Policies vary so widely that processing cannot be
a consideration.

In general, there is a great variety of titles available; there
are many adequate and fine selection aids. A list of selection
aids is found at the end of the chapter. Distribution has been
a problem in the past but is being solved by such companies as
Scholastic Book Services[3] and RECI Paperback Program of
Prentice-Hall, Inc.[4]

Selection of paperbacks is often discussed in library literature. Two good sources to have at hand when considering the
purchase of paperbacks are the two publications of John T.
Gillespie and Diana L. Spirt, *The Young Phenomenon: Paperbacks
in Our Schools*, and *Paperback Books for Young People: An Annotated Guide to Publishers and Distributors*.[5] Selection depends on
the policy of the library media staff and should be done in accordance with the approved selection policy of the school district or school building. Criteria for evaluation and selection
should be cooperatively developed (with administration, a
teacher committee, students, members of the community), ap-

proved and available in written form. (See chapter on Selection of Materials in the Library Media Center.)

In many school media centers paperbacks are integrated with the hardbound books on the shelf and cataloged just as hardbound books are. In the 1970 survey of Gillespie and Spirt it was found that from 20% to 90% of school media centers cataloged paperbacks.[6] The survey findings show that elementary schools catalog the smallest number of paperbacks, while high schools fully catalog the largest number. A comparison of the 1967 and the 1970 studies shows that cataloging of paperbacks has decreased in media centers. Judgments about this must be made in terms of the overall collection and the subject of the book, whether or not it is a duplicate copy, etc.

How to Proceed

After a study of the use of paperbacks in the school, the media specialist will make a decision in regard to each title or individual collection of paperbacks. With the rising cost of hardbound books, and since many basic titles are now available in paperback format, the expansion of the collection in paperback format should certainly be considered. Those which are to be shelved with the collection of the media center will be cataloged fully. On the other hand, a collection of recreational reading books for popular reading and for use by classes for supplementary reading will usually not be cataloged. An exception might be in the case of the very small media center collection where use demands that all materials be entered in the catalog. Paperbacks are often displayed on racks or open shelves with an ownership stamp, book pockets, and cards only. Identification of the book must be made by lettering on the cover, spine, or edge of the book. Circulation restrictions, charging system procedures, and display all influence the accessibility and the use of the paperback book. The media center should maintain a title listing of all books in paperback format if complete cataloging is not done.[7]

If the media specialist finds or considers that more bibliographic control is needed, then the paperback book must be cataloged. However, be reminded that cataloging is too expensive a procedure for mass market or low-priced titles. If some bibliographic control is needed, a shortened Dewey number and a simplified listing may be used. In any case these procedures should be followed:

Ownership stamp
Book pocket and book card
Grouping in separate collection when not cataloged

Adequate control and simplified procedures are important. Accessibility is most important. A more lenient charging policy should be considered, as well. An exchange policy is possible and has been tried in some media centers where students return a suitable paperback in place of the one they take. Losses there will be, but often they are not as extensive as anticipated; the long-term goal of reading improvement is the major consideration. A book fair or paperbacks for sale in the school are methods of distribution and for stimulating interest. Attractive and different displays create interest in the collection.

Notes

1. School Paperback Survey, 1967. School Improvement Committee of the American Association of School Librarians, American Book Publishers Council and the American Textbook Publishers Institute, *School Management* magazine, and other cooperating institutions.
2. Gillespie, John T., and Spirt, Diana L. *The Young Phenomenon: Paperbacks in Our Schools.* (Chicago: American Library Association, 1972).
3. Scholastic Book Services, 904 Sylvan Avenue, Englewood Cliffs, N.J. 07632
4. *RECI Paperback Reading Program,* a Subsidiary of Prentice-Hall, Inc. Lackawanna Avenue, West Paterson, N.J. 07424
5. Gillespie and Spirt. *The Young Phenomenon: Paperbacks in our Schools.* Gillespie, John T., and Spirt, Diana L. *Paperback Books for Young People: An Annotated Guide to Publishers and Distributors.* (Chicago: American Library Association, 1972).
6. Gillespie and Spirt. *The Young Phenomenon: Paperbacks in our Schools,* p. 15–26.
7. See also, Gillespie and Spirt. *The Young Phenomenon: Paperbacks in our Schools,* p. 72–85.

Selection Aids

General Bibliographies.

    Teacher. Monthly column, *Paperback Books.*

    Horn Book.

    Kliatt Paperback Book Guide (senior high) (Available from Kliatt, 6 Crocker Circle, West Newton, MA 02165, four times a year.)

    Library Journal. Section *Paperback Books to Come,* includes Children's Paperbacks and Adult Paperbacks.

    Publishers Weekly. Weekly *Forecasts* section includes paperback books.

Retrospective Bibliographies.

    Boylan, Lucile, and Sattler, Robert. *A Catalog of Paperbacks for Grades 7 to 12.* Metuchen, N.J.: Scarecrow Press, 1963.

    The Combined Paperback Exhibit. *Red, White and Black (and Brown and Yellow): Minorities in America.* Briarcliff Manor, N.Y., Combined Book Exhibit, 1970.

    The Combined Paperback Exhibit in Schools. (Elementary, High School, College). Briarcliff Manor, N.Y., Combined Book Exhibit, annual.

    Fader, Daniel N. and McNeil, Elton B. *Hooked on Books: Program and Proof.* New York: Putnam, 1968.

    Growing Up with Paperbacks. New York: Bowker, annual.

    The Paperback Goes to School. New York: N.Y. Bureau of Independent Publishers and Distributors, annual.

    Paperbound Book Guide for Colleges. New York: Bowker, 1972.

    Paperbound Book Guide for Elementary Schools. New York: Bowker, 1966.

    Paperbound Book Guide for High Schools. New York: Bowker, 1970.

    Paperbound Books in Print. New York: Bowker, semiannual.

    Reading is Fundamental: RIF's Guide to Book Selection. Washington, D.C.: Smithsonian Institution, 1970, with supplements.

Recommended Paperbacks. Boston: Horn Book, 1971.

Special Bibliographies.

Asia: A Guide to Paperbacks. New York: The Asia Society, 1968.

Deason, Hilary., ed. *A Guide to Science Reading.* New York: Signet, 1966.

Fleener, Charles J. and Seckinger, Ron L. *The Guide to Latin American Paperback Literature.* Gainesville, Fla.: Center for Latin American Studies, 1966.

Hershowitz, Herbert, and Marlin Bernard. *A Guide to Reading in American History: The Unit Approach.* New York: Signet, 1966.

For Further Reading

"ABPC Paperback Book Survey Sales of Mass-Market Paperback Unit Analysis—5 years 1968 vs. 1963." New York: Association of American Publishers, 1970 (mimeographed).

American Association of School Librarians. *Policies and Procedures for Selection of Instructional Materials.* Chicago: AASL, 1970.

Appleby, Bruce A. "Where the Older Kids Are." *Media & Methods* 7 (April 1970): 8.

Baur, Esther. "The Fader Plan: Detroit Style." *School Library Journal* 14 (September 15, 1967): 51–53.

Boaz, Martha. "The Enduring Quality," *ALA Bulletin* 62 (September 1968): 928–29.

Bourgeois, Yvonne, and Lilley, Dorothy. "Blueprint for Paperbacks in the High School Library." *School Library Journal* 9 (January 1963): 22–23, 25.

Davis, Joanne W. "Teaching Reading with Paperbacks in an Elementary School: Three Models for Classroom Organization." *Elementary English* 47 (December 1970): 1114–20.

Dempsey, David. "Right to Read." *Saturday Review* 54 (April 17, 1971): 22–23.

"Dr. Daniel Fader: A Child without Books Is Impoverished." *Publishers Weekly* 189 (June 20, 1968): 33–35.

Fader, Daniel N., and McNeil, Elton B. *Hooked on Books: Program and Proof.* New York: Putnam, 1968.

Falke, Mary H. "High School Students LIKE Paperbacks." *Wilson Library Bulletin* 35 (November 1960): 248–49.

Fristoe, Ashby J. "Paperbound Books—Many Problems, No Solutions." *College & Research Libraries* (September 1968): 437–42.

Grant, Annette. "Reading What They Wanna Read." *New York Times Book Review: Paperback Book Section* 7 (February 21, 1971): 8, 31.

Hall, Elvajean. "Pointers on Paperbacks." *School Library Journal* 12 (May 1966): 49–51.

Hiatt, Doris, and Klein, Celeste. "Don't Judge a Paperback by Its Cover." *Top of the News* 25 (January 1971): 171–75.

"How High Schools Use Paperback Books." *Production Information for Schools* 5 (May 1966): 36–39.

Hult, Elizabeth. "Paperbacks at Hillcrest High School." *Top of the News* 25 (June 1969): 422–25.

Kaiser, Walter H. "On the Management and Use of Paperbacks in Libraries." *Library Journal* 95 (September 15, 1970): 2875–83.

Kennedy, Tom. "Classroom Libraries—Do They Work?" *Media & Methods* 7 (April 1971): 10, 12.

Lowery, Lawrence F., and Graft, William. "Paperback Books and Reading Attitudes." *The Reading Teacher* 21 (April 1968): 618–23.

Martin, Dave. "Getting a District to Move." *Media & Methods* 7 (April 1971): 12.

Melis, Lloyd. *Survey of the Use of Paperback Books in Public Schools and Public Libraries.* Kenosha, Wis.: Carthage College, 1969.

Moon, Eric. "Editorial." *Library Journal* 91 (September 15, 1966): 4061.

Petersen, Clarence. *The Bantam Story: Twenty-five Years of Paper-back Publishing.* New York: Bantam, 1970.

Proctor, Adelaide, and Klein, Marguerite. "Paperback Pot-pourri." *Forward Magazine of Michigan Association of School Libraries* 21 (Spring 1971): 13–15.

Ross, Frank. "The Case of the Missing Paperback." *Media & Methods* 7 (April 1971): 7, 8.

Schick, Frank L. *The Paperbound Book in America.* New York: Bowker, 1958.

They Love to Read: Report on Scholastic Paperback Book Clubs in Classrooms of Five Cities. . . . New York: Scholastic Maga-zines, 1970.

XI

Serials in Microform
—other Microform Publications

The rising cost of periodicals combined with the problems of storage has forced the media specialist to evaluate patterns of purchase and storage of periodicals in the media center. The price of periodical subscriptions rose from an average of $11.66 in 1971 to $30.37 in 1979. There has been an increase of something on the order of 226% from 1969 to 1979.[1] The subscription agencies which are used by most media centers are also involved in the price squeeze and have added costs to verify and record the increased prices of periodicals. Discounts are less and are not as frequent; agency service rates climb as prices climb. Maintaining a collection of bound periodicals is prohibitively expensive and takes too much space. Periodicals collections suffer from loss and mutilation of copies, and replacement is difficult and costly.

Many university as well as school media centers are resorting to interlibrary loans to serve needs, and photocopies as requested are produced at cost to the user. MINITEX in Minnesota, WILS in Wisconsin, and Park Periodicals Service, Park College, Kansas City, Missouri, are examples of regional resources. A project in Kansas for a teletype operation of interlibrary sharing will serve this need for loan or reproduction of materials, a cooperative project between universities, public libraries, and school media centers, all in South Central Kansas. Networks can supply speedy and inexpensive copies of virtually anything.

The solution, many people believe, to the problems of handling periodicals in the future lies in microform, whether in microfiche or microfilm format. The cost of a microform of a periodical volume is roughly half that of the cost of the bound volume. It is important to have easily used readers or reader-printers that are kept in good working condition for use with microforms. It is necessary to have up to date listings or access to them through easily interpreted catalogs or computer-generated serial lists. The cost of a motorized microfilm reader can be double that of a manually operated one; a cartridge volume costs between two or three dollars more than a film of that volume on roll film. University libraries are using more and more *microfiche* from such sources as Johnson Associations, Bell and Howell, UPDATA Publications, and University Microfilms. It has significant advantages for the university library including lower cost, storage accessibility, and ease of replacement. However, for the school library media center, the *microfilm* is recommended. It is easily stored, durable, and is not easily lost or misplaced and can be used by students in the media center to provide access to easily stored periodical materials.

Here, by way of summary, are some of the main points concerning the advantages of microfilm:

> With microfilm, there are truly dramatic savings in storage space.
> Microfilm is secure, permanent, more durable than paper.
> Microfilm can save money on back issues and reprints.
> A reader-printer can make a print-out of specific pages or sections.[2]

Suggested procedure:

> Begin by using binding money for the purchase of microfilm.
> Consider microfilm first when filling gaps in your periodical collection.
> Convert your low or noncirculating backfiles to microfilm.

An example of the wide use of microfilm in the school is that of the White Plains, New York public schools where microforms are used for both independent study and as a class study tool.[3] Basic to building the broad collection in the White Plains schools was a Title II of the Elementary and Secondary Education Act grant from the New York State Department of Education. The collection includes thirty-two different periodicals on microfilm, going back in some cases to the first issue and with several sets of indexes. Sources go back as far as 1850. The collection also includes the ERIC collection of elementary books on microfiche. The media center of today must have, as learning center, a great variety of paths to knowledge.

White Plains findings about use in the secondary schools are that the most used of the periodicals titles on microfilm are:

> Atlantic Monthly
> Harper's Magazine
> Life
> Nation
> New York Times
> Newsweek
> Science
> Scientific American
> Time
> U.S. News and World Report

The ERIC fiche collection, which is available in many university and college libraries as well as in some school media centers, is not, on the whole, used as much as it should be. This collection should be available to teachers on a school-system basis and is probably not needed in every school.

To begin efficient usage of microfilm in the school situation it is necessary to demonstrate and to offer help in the operation of equipment to both students and teachers. A catalog of all serials on microfilm and of the print filed collection is a necessity. As use grows it creates an increased demand for more materials in microfilm, all of which must be added to the catalog to keep it up to date. There are many advantages both to the media center administration and to the user. Materials are always available and are in readable format. Teachers may be slower than students to begin use of microform materials, so in-service demonstrations and workshops are important. If faculty members use microfilm effectively and comfortably they will encourage greater student use.

On the elementary level, micrographics availability is limited. The Xerox Micromedia Classroom Library (XEDIA) display children's books in microfiche. All such books should also be available in the media center in hardback editions. Portable readers are now available which make the fiche a take-home reading source for students. It is an economical way to make books available for student use.

Bibliographic information on sources of microform are principally limited to the catalogs of the producers of such microforms. Many catalogs should be at hand in the professional collection as a resource for the media specialist. A new publication, "Micro-File," is proposed and should be available to list materials for grades K–12; University Microfilms and other producers of microforms have useful catalogs. A publication of value for selecting is *A Guide to Selecting Periodicals in Microform* which is published by Xerox University Microfilms and indexes 146 of the 158 titles in *Readers' Guide to Periodical Literature* plus other titles recommended by Bill Katz, a recognized authority on the periodical needs of the secondary schools, small colleges, and public libraries.[4]

The Curriculum Materials Clearinghouse (CMC) is a unique educational service of Xerox University Microfilms designed to acquire, compile, and disseminate modern instructional materials in all subject areas and at all grade levels. Its two principal purposes are:

> to provide publishing facilities for curriculum developers who have not previously considered or found a suitable means for disseminating materials
>
> to furnish the education community with fresh ideas and curriculum materials that are both practical and innovative in methodology

This latter publication in the field of education will complement the publications of the ERIC (Educational Resources Information Center) in focusing on practical instructional materials; it is not a duplication. ERIC and Curriculum Materials Clearinghouse are but two examples of the contribution which microform has to make in the future of education. There are many more possibilities.

Notes

1. Based upon *Library Journal's* Periodical Prices 1977–79 update" by F.F. Clasquin as interpreted by the American Library Association's Washington office.
2. *Journal of Micrographics* 7 (September 1973): 3.
3. Ibid., p. 6.
4. Katz, Bill, comp. *Magazines for Libraries: For the General Reader and Public, School and Junior and College Libraries,* by Bill Katz and Barry Gargal, science editor. (New York: Bowker, 1969).

For Further Reading

Clasquin, F.F. "Periodical Prices: A Three-Year Comparative Study." *Library Journal,* October 1, 1974. p. 2447–2449.

Gabriel, Michael. "Surging Serial Costs: The Microfiche Solution." *Library Journal,* October 1, 1974, p. 2451–2453.

The Journal of Micrographies: a bimonthly devoted to the science, technology, art and applications of microphotography. National Microfilm Association.

Library Technology Reports and Standards and Guidelines for Procurement of Microfilm and Microfilm Equipment, by the Libraries of the California State Universities and Colleges, adapted by the Council of Library Directors, June 22, 1973. (Available from University of California, Berkeley).

Sineath, Timothy, "Libraries and Library Subscription Agencies." *The Library Scene,* Summer 1972, p. 28–30.

Spigar, Frances G. *The Invisible Medium: The State of the Art of Microfilm and a Guide to the Literature.* ERIC Clearinghouse in Library and Information Sciences, 1973.

XII

The Professional Library
in The School

"The teachers' library is an educational investment which stimulates continuing education on the part of beginning and in-service teachers, prospective teachers, and administrators as they use its tools for a better understanding of the newer approaches to teaching and learning. It should be carefully selected, centrally located, and easily available to all teachers. Where one is already in existence, it should be strengthened, updated and improved. Where there is no library for teachers, no time should be lost in the establishment of one. If possible, one should be located in each school building where some materials will be most readily accessible to teachers, administrators and interested students. It is to be hoped that in each school system there will also be a well-developed library for teachers in the district center to supplement those in individual school buildings. Carefully-selected, well-organized and effectively used, libraries can mean well-informed, educated teachers and administrators—the surest and quickest way to our common goal of quality education."[1]

This chapter is based upon a survey of the literature, of the research findings, and upon five years experience with a functioning professional library for teachers as a part of the library media center in the school. Although there have been few evaluative studies or comments by those who have been operating professional libraries for teachers, the experience of those media specialists who maintain a well-organized professional collection is an important consideration. *Media Programs: District and School* states that "maintaining professional resources for teachers, informing them about new materials and involving them in purchasing decisions" is the responsibility of the school media program.[2] These guidelines provide criteria for the professional library on both the single-school building basis and the district/system level. The district library supplements and supports the individual building library for teachers; the collection of the district library should include those materials which it is not possible nor feasible for the individual building professional library to have in its collection, and should include works to help teachers "keep informed of trends, developments, techniques, research and experimentation in general and specialized areas of education."[3]

The professional library collection supports the educational program of its particular school, its particular teachers and administrative staff. It is the regular use of such a collection that will provide teachers with up to date and specific, direct solutions to the problems of the classroom, and the learning opportunities presented by their subject matter. This will mean books, periodicals, and examples of other media to make the newest and best of ideas and methods theirs for classroom use.

In order to use the professional library effectively, the teacher must know how to use it comfortably and easily and be inspired with a sense of need for information, and a desire to make teaching and learning more satisfying for herself and the students. The professional library makes its contribution to the school program through the enhancement of the teacher's professional skills, but it also makes a contribution to the personal development and self-realization of the teacher. Need is the key word. If the professional library fills the needs of the staff, that enthusiasm will be felt in every classroom.

Media Programs: District and School, in discussing relationship with the total media center and special considerations for the professional collection for faculty, states that it should be considered "in relation to the location of teacher's lounge, media production laboratory, department offices, main media center."[4] The professional library in the school should be close to the library media center, in a comfortable and private place in which the teacher may work among professional materials that are well selected and of *current* interest. Nothing is more dismal or more off-putting than tired, out of date material located in a dark, out-of-the way place.

Professional libraries provide an opportunity for growh and continuing updating of information for both teachers and administrators. To provide ready access to professional journals, curriculum guides from around the country, background facts, and new data for teachers to use as they discuss and consider faculty problems and instructional options, reports, and new books in each teaching field—all of this is tremendously helpful to the busy teacher. Continuing education is encouraged by the provision of such resource materials, which can be the core around which a program of workshops, seminars, and clinics is built.

The professional library provides *services* for the teacher including the securing of materials from the college or university library on an interlibrary loan basis, the preparation of bibliographies on any subject, and advice of specialists on curriculum materials. Teachers and library/media specialist confer on the selection of materials for the professional library collection, as well as on materials for the media center.

One of the persistent problems in education is the difficulty in bridging the gap between the current research findings and their application with students in the classroom. Efficiently organized materials on content and methodology are only the beginning in helping the teacher not only to keep abreast of current research but to use the knowledge effectively. The professional library can sponsor interpretation sessions which will encourage teachers in the use of all kinds of materials and methods for the enrichment of course content and the individualized assignments that provide for the needs of students of varying abilities.

The professional library will serve the administrator by giving him or her information on the basic issues surrounding daily administrative problems: the scheduling of school program, human relations among teachers, creative and innovative teaching, financing, the recruitment of teachers, personnel placement, orientation and the continuing development of staff, the role of temporary teachers, the utilization of the paraprofessional in the school building, experimental projects in the subject fields, ability grouping, special education for the handicapped and the gifted, measurement and evaluation, and policy making. In fact, every aspect of education and educational administration can be improved and approached in new ways with the application of pertinent research. Such challenges as those of maintaining good community relations can be more satisfactorily met. Ideally, some release time should be provided to teachers for individual and group work in the professional library.

The professional library is an educational investment in better teaching and learning. Where none exists, no time should be lost in establishing one.

A Plan for the Professional Library in the School

The professional library composed of books, magazines and pamphlets, and nonbook materials should be housed in a separate area adjacent to the library media center. A beginning budget for materials plus a start-up budget for equipment sufficient to make the collection fully usable within the room is required. A faculty committee should be appointed to work with the media specialist and administrator in building the collection. The professional library room (or area) is planned as one in which school and library personnel can get together to discuss problems, where teachers can work quietly, where materials may be previewed, or resource people can meet with faculty groups. The space should be flexibly arranged, with a card catalog, a vertical file, sufficient shelving for a professional book collection, study table(s) and/or individual carrels for previewing films or listening to records and tapes, and some comfortable chairs. A system of light control can enable one area to be dimmed for watching film without affecting all of the professional library area. The room will serve many functions: faculty committee meetings, viewing of new materials, selection of materials, study, and leisure reading. In sum, this is an area where the library staff and the teachers can plan the program of the school.

Adjacent to the professional library is the materials production center where equipment required for the production of specialized, tailored materials is available, either upon request to the library staff or for teacher preparation. Equipment here should include a microfilm reader-printer, a transparency maker, a photocopier, a portable overhead projector and typewriter(s). A selective listening center and microfilm readers as well as film previewers and tape recorder-players are available to teachers. A broad collection of educational reference materials would include the *Education Index* and other bibliographic sources in all subject fields. Recommended selection aids are available in the professional library for selection of all materials in both the professional library and the library media center. It is a well-organized and authoritative collection of source materials. A bibliography of suggested materials is included at the end of this chapter.

The Teacher's Library, which was a cooperative publication of the American Association of School Librarians, the National Commission for Teacher Education and Professional Standards of the National Education Association, contains case studies which might be helpful to the media specialist who is beginning to establish the professional library for teachers. It includes discussions by librarians of professional collections in various school systems: Roseville Schools, St. Paul, Minnesota; Montgomery County Public Schools, Rockville, Maryland; Broward County Public Schools, Fort Lauderdale, Florida; the public schools of Newark, New Jersey; and Lincoln Consolidated High School Library, Ypsilanti, Michigan.[5] Also listed are professional libraries in the schools which might be visited.

Organization and Administration

A professional library for teachers may be a small collection in (or near) the library media center, it may be a collection in the administrative offices of the school district, or it may be a large collection housed in a special area, but wherever it is set up and whatever its scope, a basic consideration is to determine the needs of the teaching staff and how those needs can be met. Administrative steps to the development of the plan would be:

1. Carry out a feasibility study to survey the information needs of the staff.

2. State goals and objectives for the professional library.

3. Identify existing resources within and outside the school.

4. Determine the extent of interest and build support among faculty and administration.

5. Identify potential space, staff, materials, and other budget requirements.

6. Survey available space that could be used.

7. Plan for staff involvement.

8. Schedule for establishing and opening the library collection.

9. Arrange publicity—not directed to teachers alone, but to parents and others in the community.

10. Evaluate proposed plan with various teachers, administrators, and librarians.

The size of the collection will be determined by the needs of the teaching staff and by the amount of money available. A basic start-up collection was described in *Standards for School Library Programs* (American Library Association, 1960).[6] This beginning basic collection would include:

1. A basic book collection of 200 to 1,000 titles depending upon the size and the needs of the faculty.

2. Twenty-five to fifty professional periodicals.

3. A collection of pamphlets, filmstrips, curriculun.

guides, resource units, and other special instructional materials as needed by faculty members.

4.   A minimum annual expenditure for the professional collection (over and above funds allocated for student-oriented media center materials) of $200 to $800, depending upon the size of the faculty and availability of other professional materials in the community.[7]

Regularly allocated funds for the teacher's library are most important. A yearly maintenance budget is required, as well as funds for starting the collection. The school budget is the first but not the only place to seek it. Professional gifts from teachers are a possibility, parent groups may want to make contributions, and many useful free materials are available, but these should be in addition to an operating budget item, however modest, since basic funding must come from the school budget. All gifts to the professional collection, as to any other component of the media program, should be evaluated on the same terms as purchased items.

In most cases, the professional library in the school building will be under the supervision of the media specialist in that school, assisted by an advisory committee of faculty members. Processing, circulation, and shelving of materials in the professional library collection will be handled as they are for the other parts of the media program. A professional library at the district/system level would be handled at that level by a media coordinator; perhaps in cooperation with a staff development or curriculum director at the district level.

General Guidelines

The professional library will be used by teachers who are taking graduate course work for professional improvement. The collection should be able to meet related needs in a general way. However, the needs of individual teachers for unstructured professional development in general should take

precedence over the needs of teachers taking course work because they should have access to library resources in the institutions at which they are studying. If funds are available, books
may be purchased which will support or supplement these
other resources for those teachers. Some materials need to be
purchased simply because they are controversial and to keep
teachers informed of trends in education. Teachers should expect the library to contain some books on the aspects of our
society which influence and are being influenced by education.[8]

Getting Started

The way in which the professional library is perceived by
teachers and administrators is vital. Good publicity on the part
of the planning committee and the media specialist will show
ways in which the collection can help the teacher and become
a valuable, useful tool in teaching. Teachers must be involved
in planning and in development of the professional library collection if it is to be effective. The principal must be involved
also and should actively contribute toward the creation of a
positive, enthusiastic attitude toward all of the library media
center, including, most importantly, the professional library, as
one of his significant duties. If he is a partner in the development of the professional library collection, he will promote its
use and insure adequate funding for it. Some suggestions that
may make for the excellent functioning professional library
are:

1. Involve teachers in the selection at the start and on
   a continuing basis.

2. Locate the collection conveniently and consider
   branch collections in the faculty lounge and departmental offices.

3. Assist teachers in use of the collection and help them
   with research problems.

4. Keep the entire operation open to suggestion and
   criticism.

5. Frequently bring out lists of new acquisitions, with annotations.

6. Arrange for periodic review of new books and other items.

7. Arrange displays and collections on timely themes.

8. Devise a system for routing certain materials to faculty members.

9. Bring lists of topical references to the attention of faculty groups working on a specific problem (e.g., curriculum).

10. If the teacher's library is housed in a central place, arrange for it to be available always.

11. Circulate traveling collections which may be housed in various parts of the school or schools for a period of time.[9]

How to Begin When Little Money is Available

Here are a few suggestions which have been practical and have worked:

Collect all examination copies of textbooks ordered by committees.

Collect many inexpensive pamphlets.

Send for and purchase curriculum guidelines from many school districts. (The current copy, *Curriculum Materials,* from the Association for Supervision and Curriculum Development, 1201 Sixteenth Street, N.W., Washington, D.C. 20036, is an excellent current source. It is published annually, and lists guides from many school districts.)

Collect all of the professional books from the library media center and house them in the professional library for easy access by teachers.

Ask local organizations and professional people to furnish appropriate materials when available.

Use the faculty member as an excellent source. Administrators often contribute valuable additions, professional periodicals, etc.

Process all the new materials which individual teachers or department heads purchase so that every teacher will have access to available items.

Notes

1. National Education Association; American Association of School Librarians; National Commission for Teacher Education and Professional Standards. NEA. *The Teachers' Library: How to Organize It and What To Include.* (Washington, D.C.: National Education Association, 1968), p. 7.
2. American Library Association, and Association for Educational Communications and Technology. *Media Programs: District and School.* (Chicago: American Library Association, 1975), p. 14.
3. Ibid., p. 66.
4. American Library Association, and Association for Educational Communications and Technology. *Media Programs: District and School,* p. 67, 101.
5. National Education Association, and others. *The Teachers' Library: How to Organize it and What to Include,* pp. 17–32.
6. American Association of School Librarians. *Standards for School Library Programs.* (Chicago: American Library Association, 1960), p. 24–25.
7. Ibid., p. 8.
8. Ibid., p. 12.
9. Ibid., p. 16.

Bibliography

American Association of School Libraries. *Realization: The Final Report of the Knapp School Libraries Project.* Peggy Sullivan, Editor, Knapp School Libraries Project. Chicago: American Library Association, 1968.

American Association of School Librarians. *Standards for School Library Programs.* Chicago: American Library Association, 1960.

American Library Association, and National Education Association. *Standards for School Media Programs*. Chicago: American Library Association, and Washington, D.C.: National Education Association, 1969.

Beachner, Anna M. The Librarian: Consultant in Curriculum. *School Activities and the Library*, Chicago: American Library Association, 1964.

Beggs, David W. *Decatur-Lakeview High School*. Englewood Cliffs, N.J.: Prentice-Hall, 1964.

Bergman, Winogene L. "Curriculum Libraries Are for Service, not Storage." *American School Board Journal* 151 (November 1965): 36–37.

Brown, Charles E. "This Task Is Ours." *School Library Journal*, November 1963, pp. 26–28.

Council of Chief State School Officers. *Responsibilities of State Departments of Education for School Library Services*. Washington, D.C.: The Council, 1961.

Darland, David D. "Needed: New Models for Learning to Teach." *The Journal of Teacher Education* 18 (Spring 1967): 4, 31.

Darling, Richard L. "The School Library Quarters." *Bulletin of the National Association of Secondary School Principals,* January 1966, pp. 37–44.

Darling, Richard L. "Tomorrow's Schools and Today's School Librarian." *PNLA Quarterly,* April 1964, pp. 183–188.

Detroit Public Schools. Division for the Improvement of Instruction. Department of School Libraries. A Curriculum Guide for the School Librarian in the High School. Detroit: Board of Education, 1962.

Ellsworth, Ralph E. *The School Library: Facilities for Independent Study in the Secondary School*. Stanford: Educational Facilities Laboratories, 1963.

Fenwick, Sara I., ed. *New Definitions of School Library Service*. Chicago: University of Chicago Press, 1960.

Fogarty, John. "Revolution in our Schools." *School Library Journal* 14 (January 1967): 302–303.

Gaver, Mary V., and Jones, Milbrey L. "Secondary Library Services: A Search for Essentials." *Teachers College Record* 68 (December, 1966): 200–210.

Gibbs, Wesley F. "The School Library—an Administrator Speaks." *School Activities and the Library.* Chicago: American Library Association, 1966, p. 1.

Goodlad, John I. "The Changing Curriculum of American Schools." *Saturday Review* 46 (November 16, 1963): 65–67.

Grazier, Margaret H. "Implications of the New Educational Goals for School Libraries on the Secondary Level." *Library Quarterly* 30 (January 1960): 37–46.

Henne, Frances. "The Challenge of Change." *Bulletin of the National Association of Secondary School Principles* 50 (January 1966): 75–81.

Herman, Jerry J. "The New Instructional Service Center: A New Concept?" *School Board Journal,* February 1964.

Johnson, Marvin R. "How to Plan a Good Library from Scratch." *Nation's Schools* 77, March 1966.

Library Buildings and Equipment Institute. *Planning Library Buildings for Service.* Chicago: American Library Association, 1964.

Library Buildings Institute. *Problems in Planning Library Facilities.* Chicago: American Library Association, 1964.

Lund, Kenneth W. "New Definitions in Educational Goals." *Library Quarterly* 30 (January 1960): 10–16.

McCallister, Carlyne, "Teacher Contacts with Library Important." *Education,* March 1966.

Mahar, Mary Helen, ed. *The School Library as a Materials Center.* Washington, D.C.: U.S. Government Printing Office, 1963.

McJenkin, Virginia, "Library Service to Secondary School Students." *Bulletin of the National Association of Secondary School Principals* 50 (January 1966): 10–18.

National Education Association. *The Principals Look at the Schools.* Washington, D.C.: National Education Association, 1963.

National Education Association, Project on Instruction. *Deciding What to Teach.* Washington, D.C.: National Education Association, 1963.

National Education Association, Project on Instruction. *Education in a Changing Society.* Washington, D.C.: National Education Association, 1963.

National Education Association, Project on Instruction. *Schools for the Sixties.* Washington, D.C.: National Education Association, 1963.

National Education Association. Research Division. *The Secondary-School Teacher and Library Services.* Research Monograph 1958-MI. Washington, D.C.: The Association, November, 1958.

National Education Association; American Association of School Librarians; National Commission for Teacher Education and Professional Standards, NEA. *The Teacher's Library: How to Organize It and What To Include.* Washington, D.C.: National Education Association, 1966.

The Teacher's Library: Supplement. Washington, D.C.: National Education Association, 1968.

Nicholsen, Margaret E. "The Professional Library." *Bulletin of the National Association of Secondary School Principals* 50 (January 1966): 96–106.

North Carolina Department of Public Instruction, Guidelines, *Nation's Schools* 77, March 1966.

Pate, Billy K. "Beginning and Instructional Materials Center." *Michigan Education Journal* 42 (February 1964): 30–31.

Rowell, John. "How to Tell if Your Library is Adequate." *Nation's Schools* 77, March 1966.

Schofield, Edward T. "The School Library as an Instructional Materials Center." *Maryland School Libraries* 28 (Fall 1961): 13–19.

Schwilck, Gene L. "The Library Needs a Principal." *Bulletin of the National Association of Secondary School Libraries* 50 (January 1966): 6–9.

Stone, C. Walter, "Functions of a School Library." *American School Board Journal* 15 (November 1965): 44–45.

Swarthout, Charlene R. *The School Library as Part of the Instructional System.* Metuchen, N.J.: Scarecrow Press, 1967.

Taylor, James L., and others. *Library Facilities for Elementary and Secondary Schools.* Washington, D.C.: U.S. Government Printing Office, 1965.

Trump, J. Lloyd. "Independent Study Center." *Bulletin of the National Association of Secondary School Principals* 50 (January 1966): 45–51.

Vertanes, Charles A. "Automating the School Library: An Advance Report." *Wilson Library Bulletin*, 37 (June 1963): 864–867.
Whitenack, Carolyn, ed. "New Educational Trends and Media—Their Impact on School Libraries." *ALA Bulletin*, 55 (February 1961): 117–148.

For Further Reading

AECT Materials. Association for Educational Communications and Technology, annual. (Available from AECT, 1201 16th Street N.W., Washington, D.C. 20036, or with membership in AECT).
Curriculum Materials. Association for Supervision and Curriculum Development, annual. (Available from Association for Supervision and Curriculum Development, 1201 Sixteenth Street N.W., Washington, D.C. 20036).
Davies, Ruth Ann. *The School Library: A Force for Educational Excellence.* New York: Bowker, 1969.
Gillespie, John T. and Spirt, Diana L. *Creating a School Media Program.* New York: Bowker, 1973.
Media Programs: District and School. American Library Association, and Association for Educational Communications and Technology. Chicago: American Library Association, 1975.
Realization: The Final Report of the Knapp School Libraries Project. Peggy Sullivan, Editor. American Library Association. Chicago: American Library Association, 1968.
The Teacher's Library: How to Organize It and What to Include. Washington, D.C.: National Education Association, 1966.
The Teacher's Library: How to Organize It and What to Include. 1968 edition. Washington, D.C.: National Education Association, 1968.

Appendix

Periodical Indexes

*ABRIDGED READERS' GUIDE TO PERIODICAL LITERA-
TURE.* H.W. Wilson Co., 950 University Ave., New York,
NY 10452. Monthly, Sept.–May; annual cumulations.
1936–. $10.00 yearly.

The abridged version of *Readers' Guide,* intended for
use in libraries with a limited magazine collection, indexes
approximately forty periodicals of general interest, chosen by subscribers to the index. The primary emphasis in
selection is on the reference value of the magazines, and
an effort is made to attain good subject balance so that
general interests are fairly represented. The index is
available on Talking Books, Braille, and magnetic tape
for the convenience of blind and physically handicapped
users. The annuals are cumulated biennially.

APPLIED SCIENCE AND TECHNOLOGY INDEX: a cumulative
subject index to periodicals in the fields of aeronautics,
automation, chemistry, construction, electricity and elec-
trical communication, engineering, geology and metal-
lurgy, industrial and mechanical arts, machinery, physics,
transportation, and related subjects. H.W. Wilson Co.,
950 University Ave., New York, NY 10452. Monthly,
Sept.–July; annual cumulation. 1913–57, under title of
Industrial Arts Index. 1958–. Service basis, rates on request.

ART INDEX: a cumulative author and subject index to fine arts
periodicals and museum bulletins covering archaeology,
architecture, arts and crafts, ceramics, decoration and or-
nament, graphic arts, industrial design, interior decora-

tion, landscape architecture, painting, and sculpture. H.W. Wilson Co., 950 University Ave., New York, NY 10452. Quarterly; annual and biennial cumulations. 1933–. Service basis on request.

Another in the Wilson series of indexes, *Art Index* is a guide to more than 110 United States and foreign periodicals and museums bulletins. In further amplification of the subtitle, it also covers the subjects of art history, landscape design, and photography and films.

BIOLOGICAL AND AGRICULTURAL INDEX. H. W. Wilson Co., 950 University Ave., New York NY 10452. Monthly, Oct.–Aug.; annual cumulation. 1917–64, under title of *Agricultural Index.* 1965–. Service basis on request.

This is a subject index to approximately 145 English-language periodicals covering the biological and agricultural sciences, specifically in the fields of agricultural chemicals, agricultural economics, agricultural engineering, agriculture and agricultural research, animal husbandry, biology, botany, dairying and dairy products, ecology, entomology, feeds, forestry and conservation, genetics, horticulture, microbiology, mycology, nutrition, physiology, plant science, poultry, soil science, veterinary medicine, and zoology. It should be noted, however, that the publications of the U.S. Department of Agriculture and the reports of the Agricultural Experiment Stations and Extension Services are not included, as they were in the former *Agricultural Index.*

BOOK REVIEW INDEX. Gale Research Co., 1400 Book Tower, Detroit, MI 48226. Monthly with quarterly cumulation. 1965–. $24 yearly.

Every book review in roughly 220 periodicals is indexed here. The periodicals are English-language journals, most of them American with a few British and Canadian titles; the books which they review are in the fields of general fiction, nonfiction, the humanities, the social sciences, librarianship and bibliographies, and juvenile, and each citation includes title of the books, names of authors, date of reviewing publication, name of reviewer, if signed, and page in publication.

BUSINESS PERIODICALS INDEX: a cumulative subject index
   to periodicals in the fields of accounting, advertising,
   banking and finance, general business, industries and
   trades. H. W. Wilson Co., 950 University Ave., New York
   NY 10452. Monthly except July; annual cumulation.
   1913–57, under title of *Industrial Arts Index.* 1958–. Service basis, rates on request.

   This and the *Applied Science and Technology Index* are the
   two indexes which continue the old *Industrial Arts Index.*
   Some 120 periodicals are covered in B.P.I., with a subject
   range indicated in the subtitle, and arrangement by subject heading.

Sources of Materials, Equipment, and Supplies

MOTION PICTURE & SLIDEFILM LIBRARIES

CALIFORNIA
Bailey Films
6509 De Longpre Avenue
Hollywood, CA 91506

Pyramid Films
Box 1048
Santa Monica, CA 90406

COLORADO
University of Colorado
Stadium 348
Boulder, CO 80302

CONNECTICUT
Weston Woods Films
Weston Woods, CT 06880

DISTRICT OF COLUMBIA
Bureau of Reclamation
19th & C. Streets N.W.
Washington, DC 20240

Department of State
Office of Media Services
Washington, DC 20520

Smithsonian Institution
Audio-Visual Library
Washington, DC 20560

United States Department of
Agriculture
Photo Division,
Office of Information
Washington, DC 20250

FLORIDA
Imperial Film Company
321 South Florida Avenue
Lakeland, FL 54789

ILLINOIS
Argonne National Lab
9700 South Cass Avenue
Argonne, IL 60440

Coronet Instructional Films
65 East South Water Street
Chicago, IL 60601

Encyclopaedia Britannica Films, Inc.
1150 Wilmette Avenue
Wilmette, IL 60091

Northwestern University
Film Library
828 Custer Avenue
Evanston, IL 60202

National Council of Teachers of
English
508 South Sixth Street
Champaign, IL 61820

Society for Visual Education, Inc.
1345 Diversey Parkway
Chicago, IL 60614

INDIANA
Indiana University
Audio-Visual Center
Bloomington, IN 47401

IOWA
State University of Iowa
Bureau of Audio-Visual Instruction
Iowa City, IA 52240

KANSAS
Frank Bangs Company
Box 11261
Wichita, KS 67211

University of Kansas
Bureau of Visual Instruction
Lawrence, KS 66044

MARYLAND
University of Maryland
Film Library
College Park, MD 20742

MICHIGAN
Jam Handy Organization
2821 East Grand Boulevard
Detroit, MI 48211

Western Michigan University,
Audio-Visual Center
Kalamazoo, MI 49001

MINNESOTA
World Wide Pictures
1313 Hennepin Avenue
Minneapolis, MN 55403

NEBRASKA
University of Nebraska
Bureau of Audio-Visual Instruction
Lincoln, NE 68508

NEW HAMPSHIRE
Dartmouth College Films
Fairbanks Hall
Hanover, NH 03755

NEW MEXICO
University of New Mexico
Audio-Visual Aids
Albuquerque, NM 87106

NEW YORK
American Heart Association
44 East 23rd Street
New York, NY 10010

American Petroleum Institute
1271 Avenue of Americas
New York, NY 10017

Anti-Defamation League
315 Lexington Avenue
New York, NY 10016

Association Films, Inc.
600 Madison Avenue
New York, NY 10022

Doubleday Multimedia
277 Park Avenue
New York, NY 10017

Eye-Gate House
145–601 Archer Avenue
Jamaica, NY 11435

Filmstrip House
432 Park Avenue South
New York, NY 10016

Life Filmstrips
Time and Life Building
New York, NY 10021

McGraw-Hill Films
330 West 42 Street
New York, NY 10036

Museum of Modern Art
11 West 53rd Street
New York, NY 10019

Popular Science Audio-Visual Div.
255 Lexington Avenue
New York, NY 10017

Warren Schloat Rods, Inc.
115 Tompkings
Pleasantville, NY 10570

OHIO
Twyman Films, Inc.
Box 605
Dayton, OH 45401

OKLAHOMA
University of Oklahoma
Educational Machines Service
Norman, OK 73609

TENNESSEE
University of Tennessee
Film Service
Knoxville, TN 37916

TEXAS
University of Texas
Visual Instruction Bureau
Main University
Austin, TX 78712

VERMONT
University of Vermont
Film Library and Audio-Visual
Service
Burlington, VT 05401

WISCONSIN
Milwaukee Public Museum
Audio-Visual Center
Milwaukee, WN 53203

WYOMING
University of Wyoming
Audio-Visual Services
Laramie, WY 82070

FREE FILMS
(SELECTED SOURCES)

American Automobile Association,
Department of Public Education
1712 G. Street, N.W.
Washington, DC 20006

American Iron and Steel Institute
150 East 42nd Street
New York, NY 10017

Association of American Railroads
Transportation Building
Washington, DC 20006

Bell Telephone Company
check with your local telephone
office.

General Electric Company
1 River Road
Schenectady, NY 12305

General Motors Corporation
General Motors Building
Detroit, MI 48202

Modern Talking Picture Service
3 East 54th Street
New York, NY 10022

Movies, USA
Princeton Film Center
Box 431
Princeton, NJ 08550

Sterling Educational Films
241 East 34th Street
New York, NY 10016

STILL PICTURES

Filmstrips (Silent)

Bailey Films, Inc.
5409 DeLongpre
Hollywood, CA 90028

Basic Skill Films
1355 Inverness Drive
Pasadena, CA 91103

Stanley Bowmar Company
12 Cleveland Street
Valhalla, NY 10595

Center for Mass Communications
Columbia University Press
440 West 110th Street
New York, NY 10025

Coronet Films
65 East South Water Street
Chicago, IL 60091

Educational Activities, Inc.
Box 392
Freeport, NY 11520

Encyclopaedia Britannica Films, Inc.
1150 Wilmette Avenue
Wilmette, IL 60091

Enrichment Teaching Materials
246 Fifth Avenue
New York, NY 00000

Eye-Gate House
14601 Archer Avenue
Jamaica, NY 11435

Imperial Film Company, Inc.
321 Florida Avenue
Lakeland, FL 33802

Informative Classroom Pictures
31 Ottawa Avenue
Grand Rapids, MI 49503

International Communications
Foundation
870 Monterey Pass Road
Monterey Park, CA 91754

Jam Handy Organization
2821 East Grand Blvd.
Detroit, MI 48211

McGraw-Hill Book Company
Text-Film Division
330 West 42nd Street
New York, NY 10036

Moody Institute of Science
Educational Film Division
12000 East Washington Blvd.
Whittier, CA 90606

New York Times
School Service Department
229 West 43rd Street
New York, NY 10017

Popular Science Publishing Company
355 Lexington Avenue
New York, NY 10017

Sandak, Inc.
4 East 48th Street
New York, NY 10017

Society for Visual Education
1345 East Diversey Parkway
Chicago, IL 60614

Technicolor, Inc.
1200 Frawley Drive
Costa Mesa, CA 92627

United World Films, Inc.
1445 Park Avenue
New York, NY 10029

Visual Sciences
P.O. Box 599E
Suffern, NY 10029

FILMSTRIPS
(sound)

Bailey Films, Inc.
5409 DeLongpre
Hollywood, CA 91601

Bowmar Records, Inc.
10515 Burbank Blvd.
North Hollywood, CA 90028

Cenco Educational Films
1700 Irving Park Road
Chicago, IL 60613

Coronet Films
Sales Department
Coronet Building
Chicago, IL 60614

Curtis Circulation Company
Independence Square
Philadelphia, PA 19105

DuKane Corporation
Audio-Visual Division
St. Charles, IL 60714
(This company often publishes a
complete source directory of educational sound filmstrips on both a
free-loan and purchase basis.)

Encyclopaedia Britannica Films, Inc.
1150 Wilmette Avenue
Wilmette, IL 60091

Eye-Gate House
14601 Archer Ave.
Jamaica, NY 11435

Filmstrip House, Inc.
432 Park Avenue South
New York, NY 10016

Guidance Associates
P.O. Box 5
23 Washington Ave.
Pleasantville, NY 10570
Att: L. Steves

International Communications
Foundation
870 Monterey Pass Road
Monterey Park, CA 91754

Jam Handy Organization
2821 East Grand Blvd.
Detroit, MI 48211

Life Filmstrips
Time and Life Building
Rockefeller Center
New York, NY 10021

McGraw-Hill Book Company
Text-Film Division
330 West 42nd Street
New York, NY 10036

National Film Board of Canada
680 Fifth Avenue
New York, NY 10017

2-BY 2-INCH SLIDES

American Museum of Natural
History
Central Park West at 79th Street
New York, NY 10024

Herbert E. Budek Company, Inc.
324 Union Street
Hackensack, NY 17601
(geography and art)

Clay-Adams Company, Inc.
141 East 25th Street
New York, NY 10010

Meston's Travels, Inc.
3801 North Piedras
El Paso, TX 79930

Metropolitan Museum of Art
Fifth Ave. at 82nd Street
New York, NY 10028

Musuem of Modern Art
11 West 53rd Street
New York, NY 10019

National Audubon Society
1130 Fifth Ave.
New York, NY 10028

Dr. Konrad Prothman
7 Soper Ave.
Baldwin, NY 11510

Society for Visual Education
1345 W. Diversey Parkway
Chicago, IL 60614

Ward's Natural Science Establishment, Inc.
3000 E. Ridge Road
Rochester, NY 14605

PROGRAMMED LEARNING
MATERIALS

Addison-Wesley Publishing Company
Reading, MA 01867

Allyn & Bacon, Inc.
470 Atlantic Ave.
Boston, MA 02110

American Book Co.
80 Boylston St.
Boston, MA 02116

Appleton-Century-Crofts
440 Park Ave. South
New York, NY 10016

Burgess Publishing Company
426 South Sixth Street
Minneapolis, MN 55415

Coronet Learning Programs
65 East South Water
Chicago, IL 60601

Encyclopaedia Britannica Edctl.
Corp.
425 N. Michigan
Chicago, IL 60611

Fearon Publishers
2165 Park Blvd.
Palo Alto, CA 94306

Follet Publishing Co.
1010 W. Washington Blvd.
Chicago, IL 60607

General Programmed Teaching
425 University Ave.
Palo Alto, CA 94302

Ginn & Co.
P.O. Box 191
Boston, MA 02117

Grolier Educational Corp.
Sherman Turnpike
Danbury, CT 06816 ·

Harper & Row
49 East 33 St.
New York, NY 10016

Holt, Rinehart & Winston
383 Madison Ave.
New York, NY 10017

Harcourt, Brace & Jovanovich
757 Third Ave.
New York, NY 10017

J.B. Lippincott Co.
East Washington Square
Philadelphia, PA 19105

McGraw-Hill Book Co. Inc.
330 W. 42 Street
New York, NY 10036

Prentice-Hall, Inc.
Englewood Cliffs, NJ 07632

Scholastic Magazines, Inc.
50 West 44 Street
New York, NY 10036

Science Research Associates, Inc.
259 E. Erie
Chicago, IL 60611

Xerox Education Division
600 Madison Ave.
New York, NY 10022

RECORDED INSTRUCTIONAL
MATERIAL

Bowmar Records
622 Rodier Drive
Mundelein, IL 60060

Enrichment Teaching Materials
246 Fifth Ave.
New York, NY 10001

Folkways/Scholastic Records
906 Sylvan Avenue
Englewood Cliffs, NJ 07632

Great Plains Instructional
TV Library
University of Nebraska
Lincoln, NE 68508

Gregg Division
McGraw-Hill Book Company
330 West 42 Street
New York, NY 10036

Imperial Production, Inc.
247 W. Court Street
Kankakee, IL 70901

National Instructional TV Center
Box A
Bloomington, IN 47401

Spoken Arts, Inc.
59 Locust Ave.
New Rochelle, NY 10801

Memorex Precision Magnetic Tape
1180 Shulman Ave.
Santa Clara, CA 95050

RCA
Camden, NJ 08101

AUDIOVISUAL EQUIP-MENT/RECORD PLAYERS

Allied Radio Corporation
100 N. Western Ave.
Chicago, IL 60612

Bogen Company
Division of the Siegler Corporation
Paramus, NJ 07652

Newcomb Audio Products Company
12881 Bradley Ave.
Sylimar, CA 91342

RCA Victor Division
Radio Corporation of America
Camden, NJ 08102

Rheem Califone Corporation
1020 N. La Brea Ave.
Hollywood, CA 90028

TAPE RECORDERS

Ampex
401 Broadway
Redwood City, CA 94063

Bell and Howell Company
7100 McCormick Road
Chicago, IL 60645

RCA Victor Division
Radio Corporation of America
Camden, NJ 08102

Rheem Califone Corporation
1020 N. La Brea Ave.
Hollywood, CA 90028

Sony Corporation of America
Sun Valley, CA 91352

Webcor, Inc.
5610 W. Bloomingdale Ave.
Chicago, IL 60639

FILMSTRIP PROJECTORS (SILENT)

American Optical Company
Eggert and Sugar Roads
Buffalo, NY 14215

Bell and Howell Company
7100 McCormick Road
Chicago, IL 60645

Eastman Kodak Company
343 State Street
Rochester, NY 14608

Graflex Inc.
3750 Monroe Ave.
Rochester, NY 14603

Viewlex Company, Inc.
Holbrook, L.I., NY 11741

FILMSTRIP PROJECTORS (SOUND)

Audio-Master Corporation
17 E. 45th Street
New York, NY 10017

DuKane Corporation
St. Charles, IL 60174

LaBelle Industries, Inc.
522 S. Washington Street
Oconomowoc, WI 53066

Viewlex Company, Inc.
Holbrook, L.I., NY 11741

2-BY 2-INCH SLIDE
(PROJECTORS)

Argus Cameras, Inc.
Ann Arbor, MI 48103

Bausch and Lomb Optical Company
626 St. Paul Street
Rochester, NY 14605

Bell and Howell Company
7100 McCormick Road
Chicago, IL 60645

Eastman Kodak Company
343 State Street
Rochester, NY 14650

Graflex, Inc.
3570 Monroe Ave.
Rochester, NY 14603

E. Leitz, Inc.
46 Park Ave. South
New York, NY 10016

Viewlex Company, Inc.
Holbrook, L.I., NY 11741

16MM SOUND PROJECTORS

Bell and Howell Company
7100 McCormick Road
Chicago, IL 60645

Eastman Kodak Company
343 State Street
Rochester, NY 14650

Graflex, Inc.
3750 Monroe Ave.
Rochester, NY 14603

RCA Victor Division
Radio Corporation of America
Camden, NJ 08102

Rheem Califone Corporation
1020 N. La Brea Ave.
Hollywood, CA 90028

8MM SOUND PROJECTORS

Bell and Howell Company
7100 McCormick Road
Chicago, IL 60645

Eastman Kodak Company
343 State Street
Rochester, NY 14650

OPAQUE PROJECTORS

American Optical Company
Eggert and Sugar Roads
Buffalo, NY 14215

Bausch and Lomb Optical Company
85731 St. Paul Street
Rochester, NY 14605

Charles Beseler Company
219 S. 18th Street
East Orange, NJ 07018

OVERHEAD AND STANDARD
LANTERN-SLIDE PROJECTORS

American Optical Company
Eggert and Sugar Roads
Buffalo, NY 14215

Bausch and Lomb Optical Company
626 St. Paul Street
Rochester, NY 14605

Charles Beseler Company
219 S. 18th Street
East Orange, NJ 07018

3M Company
2501 Hudson Road
St. Paul, MN 55119

TELEVISION RECEIVERS
(SCHOOL MODELS)

Admiral Corporation
3800 W. Cortland Street
Chicago, IL 60647

General Electric Company
Receiver Division
600 Old Liverpool Road
Liverpool, NY 13088

RCA Victor Division
Radio Corporation of America
Front and Cooper Streets
Camden, NJ 08102

Sony Corporation
47-47 Van Dam Street
Long Island City, NY 11101

LISTENING LABORATORIES

Audio Teaching Center
137 Hamilton Street
New Haven, CT 06511

Hamilton Electronics Corporation
2726 W. Pratt Ave.
Chicago, IL 60645

Maico Corporation
21 N. Third Street
Minneapolis, MI 48071

Radio Corporation of America
Front and Cooper Streets
Camden, NJ 08102

Westinghouse Electric Corporation
P.O. Box J
Sea Cliff, NY 11579

White Electronic Development
Corporation
1180 Avenue of the Americas
New York, NY 10036

VIDEOTAPE RECORDERS

Ampex
401 Broadway
Redwood City, CA 94063

Panasonic/Matsushita Electric
Corporation
200 Park Ave.
New York, NY 10017

Sony Corporation
47-47 Van Dam Street
Long Island City, NY 11101

Westinghouse Electric Corporation
P.O. Box J
Sea Cliff, NY 11579

TEACHING MACHINES

Welch Scientific Company
7300 N. Linder Ave.
Skokie, IL 60076

TRANSPARENCIES &
PREPARATION MATERIALS

Denoyer-Geppert Co.
5235 Ravenswood Ave.
Chicago, IL 60640

Educational Audio Visual, Inc.
Pleasantville, NY 10570

Keuffel & Esser Co.
20 Whippany Road
Morristown, NJ 07960

Laidlaw Bros.
Thatcher & Madison River
Forest, IL 60305

3M Company Visual Productions
2501 Hudson Road
St. Paul, MN 55119

Tweedy Transparencies
208 Hollywood Ave.
East Orange, NJ 07018

United Transparencies
Box 888
Binghamton, NY 13902

MATERIALS FOR MAKING
TRANSPARENCIES

Charles Beseler Company
213 S. 18th Street
East Orange, NJ 07018

Instructo Products Company
1635 N. 55th Street
Philadelphia, PA 19131

Keuffel and Esser Company
300 Adams Street
Hoboken, NJ 07030

Ozalid Division
General Aniline and Film
Coproration
140 W. 51st Street
New York, NY 10020

Printing Arts Research
Laboratories, Inc.
Arcada Building
Santa Barbara, CA 93104

Tecnifax Corporation
195 Appleton Street
Holyoke, MA 01040

3M Company
Visual Products
2501 Hudson Road
St. Paul, MN 55119

Varityper Corporation
720 Frelinghuysen Ave.
Newark, NJ 07114

COMMERCIAL TRANSPARENCIES

Allyn & Bacon, Inc.
AV Department
150 Tremont Street
Boston, MA

Creative Visuals
P.O. Box 310
Big Spring, TX 79720

Encyclopaedia Britannica Films, Inc.
1150 Wilmette Ave.
Wilmette, IL 60091

Ginn & Co.
Arlington Heights, IL 60005

C. S. Hammond and Company
515 Valley Street
Maplewood, NJ 07040

Keuffel and Esser Company
300 Adams Street
Hoboken, NJ 07030

McGraw-Hill Book Company
TextFilm Division
330 W. 42nd Street
New York, NY 10036

Popular Science Publishing Company
Audio-Visual Division
355 Lexington Ave.
New York, NY 10027

Rand McNally & Company
P.O. Box 372
Chicago, IL 60645

Science Research Associates, Inc.
E. Erie Street
Chicago, IL 60611

3M Company
Visual Products
2501 Hudson Road
St. Paul, MN 55119

United Transparencies, Inc.
P.O. Box 888
Binghamton, NY 13903

Visual Materials, Inc.
980 O'Brien Drive
Menlo Park, CA 94025

TELEVISION
GENERAL INFORMATION

Committee on Television
American Council on Education
1785 Massachusetts Ave. N.W.
Washington, D.C. 20036

Department of Audiovisual
Instruction
National Education Association
1201 Sixteenth Street N.W.
Washington, D.C. 20036

Educational Television and
Radio Center
New York, NY 10036

National Association of Educational
Broadcasters
1346 Connecticut Avenue, N.W.
Washington, DC

Net Film Service
Indiana University
Bloomington, IN 47401

TELEVISION NETWORKS

American Broadcasting Company
7 W. 66th Street
New York, NY 10023

Columbia Broadcasting System
485 Madison Ave.
New York, NY 10022

Educational Television and
Radio Center
New York, NY 10036

National Broadcasting Company
30 Rockefeller Plaza
New York, NY 10020

TELEVISION RECEIVERS

EmersonNY-NJ Inc.
4 Empire Blvd
Moonachie, NJ 07465

Admiral Corp.
3800 Cortland Street
Chicago, IL 60647

General Electric Co.
Electronics Park
Syracuse, NY 13201

Magnavox, Inc.
Bueter Road
Fort Wayne, IN 46806

Motorola Consumer Products
9401 Grand Ave.
Franklin Park, IL 60131

Philco-Ford Corp.
Tiaga & C Streets
Philadelphia, PA 19134

RCA
Camden, NJ 08101

Sony Corp. of America
47-47 Van Dam Street
Long Island City, NY 11101

Sylvania
730 Third Ave.
New York, NY 10017

Westinghouse
200 Park Ave.
New York, NY 10017

Zenith Sales Corp.
1900 North Austin
Chicago, IL 60639

RADIO NETWORKS

American Broadcasting Company
7W. 66th Street
New York, NY 10023

Columbia Broadcasting System
485 Madison Ave.
New York, NY 10022

Mutual Broadcasting System
1440 Broadway
New York, NY 10018

National Broadcasting Company
30 Rockefeller Plaza
New York, NY 10020

DISK RECORDINGS

American Library Association
50 E. Huron Street
Chicago, IL 60611

Bowmar Records
10515 Burbank Blvd.
N. Hollywood, CA 91601

Caedmon Records
461 Eighth Ave.
New York, NY 10001

Capitol Records
Sunset Blvd. and Vine Street
Hollywood, CA 90028

Columbia Records, Educational
Division
799 Seventh Ave.
New York, NY 10019

Decca Records, Inc.
50 W. 57th Street
New York, NY 10019

Educational Recording Services
5922 Abernathy Drive
Los Angeles, CA 90045

Enrichment Teaching Materials, Inc.
246 Fifth Ave.
New York, NY 10001

Folkways Records and Service
Corporation
50 W. 44th Street
New York, NY 10036

National Council of Teachers of
English
704 S. Sixth Street
Champaign, IL 61820

RCA Victor Division, Radio Corpora-
tion of America,
Educational Services
Camden, NJ 08102

Spoken Arts, Inc.
59 Locust Ave.
New Rochelle, NY 10801

H. Wilson Corporation
546 W. 119th Street
Chicago, IL 60628

CAMERAS AND ACCESSORIES
MOTION PICTURE & STILL

Bell & Howell
7100 McCormick Road
Chicago, IL 60645

Eastman Kodak Co.
343 State Street
Rochester, NY 14608

Lafayette Radio & Electronics
111 Jericho Tpk.
Syosset, NY 11791

Polaroid Corp.
549 Technology Sq.
Cambridge, MA 02139

PHOTOGRAPHY
STILL CAMERAS

Allied Impex Corporation
300 Park Ave. South
New York, NY 10010

Argus Cameras, Inc.
5950 W. Touhy
Chicago, IL 60648

Bell and Howell Company
7100 McCormick Road
Chicago, IL 60695

Charles Beseler Company
219 S. 18th Street
East Orange, NJ 07018

Eastman Kodak Company
343 State Street
Rochester, NY 14608

Konica Camera Corporation
Box 1070
Woodside, NY 11377

E. Leitz, Inc.
46 Park Ave. South
New York, NY 10016

Minolta Corporation
200 Park Ave. South
New York, NY 10003

Nikon, Inc.
Garden City, NY 11533

Polaroid Corporation
549 Technology Sq.
Cambridge, MA 02138

Yashica
50-17 Queens Blvd.
Woodside, NY 11377

Carl Zeiss, Inc.
485 Fifth Ave.
New York, NY

MOTION-PICTURE CAMERAS

Allied Impex Corporation
300 Park Ave. South
New York, NY 10010

Bell and Howell Company
7100 McCormick Road
Chicago, IL 60645

Eastman Kodak Company
343 State Street
Rochester, NY 14608

Minolta Corporation
200 Park Ave. South
New York, NY 10003

DEALERS—AV SUPPLIES

Frank Bangs Co.
231 Ida, Box 11261
Wichita, KS 67211

Library Filmstrip Center
3033 Aloma
Wichita, KS 67211

Steve Smith Cameras
Box 1216
Topeka, KS 66601

Jim Handy Products
2821 East Grand Blvd.
Detroit, MI 48211

Hoover Bros.
1415 So. Big Bend Blvd.
St. Louis, MO 63117

Twyman Films
329 Salem Ave.
Dayton, OH 45406

FILM RAW STOCK

3M Company
2501 Hudson Road
St. Paul, MN 55119

PRODUCERS—FILMS,
FILMSTRIPS, SLIDES

Library Filmstrip Center
3033 Aloma
Wichita, KS 67211

PHOTOCOPYING & DUPLICATING
MACHINES & SUPPLIES

Addressograph Multigraph
1200 Babbit Road
Cleveland, OH 44132

Dick, A. B., Company
5700 W. Touhy Avenue
Chicago, IL 69648

Eastman Kodak Company
343 State Street
Rochester, NY 14650

3M Company
2501 Hudson Road
St. Paul, MN 55119

SCIENTIFIC INSTRUMENTS &
LAB EQUIPMENT

Houghton Mifflin Company
110 Tremont Street
Boston, Mass. 02107

TAPE RECORDERS & PLAYBACKS

Radio Corp. of America
Camden, NJ 08101

Rheem Califone Corp.
5922 Bowcroft Street
Los Angeles, CA 90064

Sony-Superscope, Inc.
47-47 Van Dam Street
Long Island City, NY 11101

Telex
9600 Aldrich Ave. S.
Minneapolis, MN 55420

Wollensak/3M Company
2501 Hudson Road
St. Paul, MN 55114

PRERECORDED TAPES

Educational Development
Laboratories
Huntington, NY 11743

Heath, de Rochemont Corp.
9 Newbury Street
Boston, MA 02116

National Association of Educational
Broadcasters
14 Gregory Hall, University of
Colorado
Boulder, CO 80302

Radio Shack
730 Commonwealth Ave.
Boston, MA 02215 or
1515 So. University Drive
Ft. Worth, TX 76107

Spoken Arts, Inc.
59 Locust Ave.
New Rochelle, NY 10801

World Tapes for Education
Box 9211
Dallas, TX 75215

MAPS AND GLOBES

Denoyer-Geppert Co.
5235 Ravenswood Ave.
Chicago, IL 60604

Encyclopedia Britannica
425 No. Michigan
Chicago, IL 60611

Field Enterprises Edu. Corp.
510 Mdse. Mart Plaza
Chicago, IL 60618

Rand McNally & Co.
Box 7600
Chicago, IL 60078

Professional Organizations

1. *American Educational Research Association,* 1126 Sixteenth
   Street, N.W., Washington, DC 20036.
Divisions of this organization of behavioral scientists and ed-
ucators interested in development, application, and improve-
ment of educational research are: Administration, Curriculum
and Objectives, Instruction and Learning, Measurement and
Research Methodology, Counseling and Human Development,
History and Historiography, Social Context of Education, and
School Evaluation and Program Development.
   Publications: *Educational Researcher, Review of Educational Research, American Educational Research Journal, Handbook of Research on Teaching.*

2. *American Library Association,* 50 E. Huron Street, Chicago,
   IL 60611.
Membership open to persons interested in extending and
improving library media information service and librarianship
in the United States and throughout the world.
   Publications: *American Libraries,* the official journal of ALA;
Booklist, Choice and *Choice Reviews-on-Cards, Library Technology
Reports.* In addition many of the divisions publish journals, in-
cluding: *College and Research Libraries, Library Resources and
Technical Services, School Media Quarterly, Top of the News,* the
Journal of Library Automation, and *JOLA Technical Communications.*

3. *Association for Education Communications and Technology,*
   1126 Sixteenth Street, N.W., Washington, DC 20036.

The AECT is trying to improve instruction through effective use of educational technology. Teacher educators, audiovisual and instructional materials specialists, educational technologists, instructional development specialists, audiovisual and television production personnel make up the membership. AECT divisions are segments of the membership organized to represent major educational communications and technology professional interest areas.

Publications: *Audiovisual Instruction;* the quarterly journal, *AV Communication Review;* a monthly newsletter, ECT.

4. *Association of Chief State School Audio-Visual Officers* (ACSS-AVO), State Department of Instruction, 1333 W. Camelback Rd., Phoenix, Az 85013.

Members are representatives of state departments of education who are in charge of programs and activities associated with the use of audiovisual media in schools in the state.

5. *Association for Educational Systems* (AEDS), 1201 Sixteenth Street, N.W., Washington, DC 20036

Members are interested in systems development. Publication is *AEDS Monitor.*

6. *Association for Supervision and Curriculum Development* (ASCD), 1201 Sixteenth Street, N.W., Washington, DC 20036.

Professional organization of supervisors, curriculum, coordinators, directors of curriculum, consultants, professors of education, classroom teachers, principals, and others interested in school improvement at all levels of education. A department of the National Education Association.

Publications include: *Educational Leadership, Yearbook, News Exchanges,* as well as several books through the year.

7. *Educational Film Library Association* (EFLA), 17 W. Sixtieth Street, New York, NY 10023.

Membership includes schools, colleges, public libraries, church groups, labor organizations, film producers, distributors, and individuals. Founded in 1943, EFLA serves as the national clearinghouse of information about films, including their production, distribution, and use.

Publications: *American Film Festival Guide,* special mono-graphs and reports, and film bibliographies on selected topics. Access to reference files of EFLA and advisory service.

8. *Film Library Information Council* (FLIC), 17 W. Sixtieth Street, New York, NY 10023.

Organized in 1967, the Film Library Information Council identifies as its major purposes those of getting the best, the most stirring, the most provocative films in use at the commu-nity level, and of working with other oganizations to promote greater film use by libraries. *Film Library Quarterly* is FLIC's of-ficial journal.

9. *National Association of Educational Broadcasters* (NAEB), 1346 Connecticut Avenue, N.W., Washington, DC 20036.

This association is concerned primarily with radio and tele-vision. Today it is more interested in the personal effects of media or with broadcasting per se.

Publishes *NAEB Newsletter* and the bimonthly *Educational Broadcasting Review.*

10. *National Association of Language Laboratory Directors* (NALLD), Box E, Brown University, Providence, RI 02912.

Membership includes anyone whose interests bring him into working contact with the administration or operation of any machine-aided language learning program in an educational institution or governmental agency.

Publication: *NALLD Journal.* The publications center is a free service to NALLD members.

11. *National Society for Programmed Instruction* (NSPI), P.O. Box 137 Cardinal Station, Washington, DC 20044.

The preparation and use of programmed learning materials for schools, industry, the military, government, and health sci-ences are the concerns of members.

Publications include: *NSPI Newsletter, NSPI Journal,* and *NSPI Official International Directory of Members.*

12. *University Film Association* (UFA), Audiovisual Center, Dart-mouth College, Hanover, NH 03755.

Membership of the association includes writers, editors, directors, cameramen, and technicians producing educational, documentary, scientific, and public relations films in colleges and universities. Purposes include promoting an interest in the training and professionalism of film producers in universities, providing a forum for exchange of ideas within this group and with other groups whose interests relate to film production, screening, and evaluating university-produced films, and recording developments and activities in the field.

Official publications include *Journal of the University Film Association* and a *Newsletter of the University Film Association*.

Directory of Publishers
and Distributors

A.L.A. American Library Association, Publishing Services
50 E. Huron Street
Chicago, IL 60611

Abingdon. Abingdon Press, Hdqrs.
201 8th Ave. South
Nashville, TN 37210

Am. Assn. for the Advancement of Science. American Association for the
Advancement of Science
1515 Massachusetts Ave. N.W.
Washington, DC 20005

Am. Heritage Press. See McGraw

Atheneum Pubs. Atheneum Publishers
122 E. 42nd Street
New York, NY 10017

Barrons Educ. Serv. Barron's Educational Series, Inc.
113 Crossways Park Drive
Woodbury, NY 11797

Beacon Press. Beacon Press, Inc.
25 Beacon Street
Boston, MA 02108

Bobbs. The Bobbs Merrill Company, Inc.
4300 W. 62nd. Street
Indianapolis, IN 46206

Bowker. The R. R. Bowker Company, Xerox Education Group
1180 Ave. of the Americas
New York, NY 10036

Collier Bks. See Macmillan Pub. Co.

Columbia Univ. Press. Columbia University Press
562 W. 113th Street
New York, NY 10025

Congressional Quarterly. Congressional Quarterly, Inc.
1735 K Street, N.W.
Washington, DC 20006

Cornell Univ. Press. Cornell University Press
124 Roberts Pl
Ithaca, NY 14850

Coward, McCann & Geoghegan. Coward, McCann & Geoghegan, Inc.
200 Madison Ave.
New York, NY 10016

Crowell. Thomas Y. Crowell Company
666 5th Ave.
New York, NY 10019

Crowell-Collier Press. See Macmillan Pub. Co.

Crown. Crown Publishers, Inc.
419 Park Ave. South
New York, NY 10016

Day. The John Day Company, Inc.
257 Park Ave. South
New York, NY 10010

Delacorte Press. Delacorte Press, 1 Dag Hammarskjold Plaza
245 E. 47th Street
New York, NY 10017

Dial Press. The Dial Press, 1 Dag Hammarskjold Plaza
245 E. 47th Street
New York, NY 10017

Dodd. Dodd, Mead & Company
79 Madison Ave.
New York, NY 10016

Dolphin Bks. Dolphin Books
277 Park Ave.
New York, NY 10017

Doubleday. Doubleday & Company, Inc.
245 Park Ave.
New York, NY 10017

Dutton. E. P. Dutton & Company, Inc.
201 Park Ave. South
New York, NY 10003

Educ. Film Lib. Assn. Educational Film Library Association, Inc.
17 W. 60th Street
New York, NY 10023

Encyclopaedia Britannica. Encyclopaedia Britannica Educational Corporation
    (Encyclopaedia Press)
425 N. Michigan Ave.
Chicago, IL 60611

Farrar, Straus. Farrar, Straus & Giroux, Inc.
19 Union Sq. West
New York, NY 10003

Follett. Follett Publishing Company
1010 W. Washington Blvd.
Chicago, IL 60607

Four Winds. The Four Winds Press
50 W. 44th Street
New York, NY 10036

Funk. Funk & Wagnalls Publishing Company, Inc.
606 5th Ave.
New York, NY 10019

Gale Res. Gale Research Company
700 Book Tower
Detroit, MI 48226

Glencoe Press. Glencoe Press
8701 Wilshire Blvd.
Beverly Hills, CA 90211

Good Housekeeping Bks. Good Housekeeping Books
250 W. 55th Street
New York, NY 10019

Grosset. Grosset & Dunlap, Inc.
51 Madison Ave.
New York, NY 10010

Hammond Almanac. See Hammond

Harcourt. Harcourt, Brace Johanovich, Inc.
757 3rd Ave.
New York, NY 10017

Harper. Harper & Row, Publishers
10 E. 53rd Street
New York, NY 10022

Hawthorn Bks. Hawthorn Books, Inc.
260 Madison Ave.
New York, NY 10016

Hill & Wang. Hill & Wang
19 Union Sq. West
New York, NY 10003

Holt. Holt, Rinehart and Winston, Inc.
383 Madison Ave.
New York, NY 10017

Houghton. Houghton Mifflin Company
2 Park Street
Boston, MA 02107

Knopf. Alfred A. Knopf, Inc.
201 E. 50th Street
New York, NY 10022

Libs. Unlimited. Libraries Unlimited, Inc.
Box 236
Littleton, CO 80120

Little. Little, Brown and Company
34 Beacon Street
Boston, MA 02106

Lothrop. Lothrop, Lee & Shepard Company
105 Madison Ave.
New York, NY 10016

MIT Press. Massachusetts Institute of Technology Press
28 Carleton Street
Cambridge, MA 02142

McGraw. McGraw-Hill Book Company
1221 Avenue of the Americas
New York, NY 10020

McKay. David McKay Company, Inc.
2 Park Ave.
New York, NY 10016

Macmillan Pub. Co. Macmillan Publishing Company, Inc.
866 3rd Ave.
New York, NY 10022

Macrae Smith Co. Macrae Smith Company, Lewis Tower Bldg.
225 S. 15th Street
Philadelphia, PA 19102

Merriam. G. & C. Merriam Company
47 Federal Street
Springfield, MA 01101

Messner. Julian Messner
1230 Ave. of the Americas
New York, NY 10020

Morrow. William Morrow & Company, Inc., Publishers
105 Madison Ave.
New York, NY 10016

Natl. Council of Teachers of English. National Council of Teachers of English
1111 Kenyon Rd.
Urbana, IL 68101

Natl. Geographic Soc. National Geographic Society
17 & M Streets, N.W.
Washington, DC 20036

New Am. Lib. The New American Library, Inc.
1301 Avenue of the Americas
New York, NY 10019

Norton. W. W. Norton & Company, Inc., Publishers
500 5th Ave.
New York, NY 10036

Oceana. Oceana Publications, Inc.
75 Main Streets
Dobbs Ferry, NY 10522

Oxford. Oxford University Press, Inc.
200 Madison Ave.
New York, NY 10016

Parents' Mag. Press. Parents' Magazine Press
52 Vanderbilt Ave.
New York, NY 10017

Penguin. Penguin Books, Inc.
7110 Ambassador Red
Baltimore, MD 21207

Praeger. Praeger Publishers, Inc.
111 4th Ave.
New York, NY 10003

Prentice-Hall. Prentice-Hall, Inc.
Route 9W
Englewood Cliffs, NJ 07632

Princeton Univ. Press. Princeton University Press
Princeton, NJ 08540

Putnam. G. P. Putnam's Sons
200 Madison Ave.
New York, NY 10016

Rand McNally. Rand McNally & Company
Box 7600
Chicago, IL 60680

Random House. Random House, Inc.
201 E. 50th Street
New York, NY 10022

Regnery. Henry Regnery Company
111 W. Illinois Street
Chicago, IL 60610

Richards Rosen Press. Richards Rosen Press, Inc.
29 E. 21st Street
New York, NY 10010

Saturday Review Press. See Dutton

Scribner. Charles Scribner's Sons
597 5th Ave.
New York, NY 10017

Shoe String. The Shoe String Press, Inc.
995 Sherman Ave.
Hamden, CT 06514

Silver. Silver Burdett Company
250 James Street
Morristown, NJ 07960
Distributor of Time-Life Books to schools and libraries

Simon & Schuster. Simon & Schuster, Inc., Publishers
630 5th Ave.
New York, NY 10020

Smithsonian Inst. Press
Washington, DC 20560

Stackpole Bks. Stackpole Books
Cameron & Kelker Streets
Harrisburg, PA 17105

Sterling. Sterling Publishing Company, Inc.
419 Park Ave.
New York, NY 10016

Sunrise Bks. See Dutton

Supt. of Docs. Superintendent of Documents
Government Printing Office
Washington, DC 20402

Taplinger. Taplinger Publishing Company, Inc.
200 Park Ave., South
New York, NY 10003

Time, Inc. Time, Inc., Book Division
Time & Life Bldg., Rockefeller Center
New York, NY 10020
  See also Silver

Time-Life Bks. See Time Inc.

Trident Press. Trident Press
630 5th Ave.
New York, NY 10020

Twayne. See Hall, G.K. & Co.

Univ. of Chicago Press. University of Chicago Press
5801 Ellis Ave.
Chicago, Il 60637

Univ. of Neb. Press. University of Nebraska Press
901 N. 17th Street
Lincoln, NB 68508

Van Nostrand-Reinhold. Van Nostrand-Reinhold Company
450 W. 33rd Street
New York, NY 10001

Viking. The Viking Press, Inc.
625 Madison Ave.
New York, NY 10022

Walck, H.Z. Henry Z. Walck, Inc. Publishers
750 3rd Ave.
New York, NY 10017

Watson-Guptill. Watson-Guptill Publications
1 Astor Plaza
New York, NY 10036

Watts, F. Franklin Watts, Inc.
730 5th Ave.
New York, NY 10019

Wilson, H.W. The H. W. Wilson Company
950 University Ave.
Bronx, NY 10452

Glossary of Terms[1]

Accession. (n.) A book or other similar material acquired by a library for its collections. (v.) To record books and other similar material added to a library in the order of acquisition.

Acquisition Departments. The administrative unit in charge of selecting and acquiring books, periodicals, and other material by purchase, exchange, and gift, and keeping the necessary records of these additions. Sometimes referred to as Order Department or Accession Department.

Admission Record. A permit, pass, for gaining admission to a school library with a record of the student's classroom and study hall schedules. Also called Admission Slip, Library Pass, Library Permit, and Permit.

Alphabetizing or Alphabeting. Arranging in alphabetical order.

Analytical Entry. The entry of some part of a work or of some article contained in a collection (volume of essays, serial, etc.), including a reference to the publications which contains the article or work entered.

   In special libraries it may be an entry for a significant paragraph, section, table, etc., or for a single statement or figure.

Annotation. 1. A note that describes, explains, or evaluates; especially such a note added to an entry in a bibliography, reading list, or catalog. Sometimes called Book Note.

   2. The process of making such notes.

Annual. 1. A publication issued regularly once a year, as an annual report or proceedings of an organization; or, a yearly publication that reviews events or developments during a year, sometimes limited to a special field. 2. A giftbook. (q.v.)

Author Card. A catalog card containing an author entry.

Authority File or List. An official list of forms selected as headings in a catalog, giving for author and corporate names and for the forms of entry of anonymous classics the sources used for establishing the forms, together with the variant forms. If the list is a name list, it is sometimes called the Name List or Name File.

Bibliography. 1. The study of the material form of books, with comparison of variations in some issues of copies, as a means of determining the history and transmission of texts. 2. The art of describing books correctly with respect to authorship, editions, physical forms, etc. 3. The preparations of lists of books, maps, etc. 4. A list of books, maps, etc., differing from a catalog in not being necessarily a list of materials in a collection, a library, or a group of libraries.

Book Jacket. A detachable wrapper, plain or printed, flush with the covers at head and tail, but folded over between the cover, both front and back and the book proper. Also called Dust Wrapper, Jacket, Jacket Cover, and Wrapper.

Book Number. A combination of letters and figures used to arrange books in the same classification of an author number and a work mark. Occasionally called a Book Mark.

Book Selection. 1. The process of choosing books for library collections. 2. A library school course on the principles underlying the choices of material for various kinds of libraries and types of readers.

Book Pocket. A pocket of stiff paper, an envelope, or a slip of paper, pasted on the inside of a book cover to hold a book card or a borrower's card. Also called Card Pocket and Pocket.

Broad Classification. Arrangement of subjects in a classification system in a broad general divisions with a minimum of subdivisions.

Brochure. A short printed work, consisting of only a few leaves, merely stitched together with thread or cord and not otherwise bound. Literally, a stitched work (from the French *brocher*, to stitch).

Call Number. Letters, figures, and symbols, separate or in combination, assigned to a book and a book number. Sometimes known as Call Mark.

Card Catalog. A catalog in which entries are on separate cards arranged in a definite order in drawers.

Card Number. *(Catalog Cards.)* A number, or a combination of a letter, letters, or a date and a number, that identifies a particular card in a stock of printed catalog cards, such as Library of Congress cards.

Card Tray. A drawer for holding cards in a card cabinet. Also called Card Drawer, and in a card catalog case, Catalog Drawer and Catalog Tray.

Carrel (Carrell.) An alcove for individual study in a library stack, formed by partitions or arrangement of shelving. Also called Cubicle or Stall.

Central Shelf List. A shelf list of the main library of a library system. Sometimes called Main Shelf List. A combined shelf list of books in a main library and its branches or a system of school libraries. Also called Union Shelf List.

Centralized Cataloging. 1. The preparation in one library or a central agency of catalogs for all the libraries of a system. 2. The preparation of catalog cards by one library or other agency which distributes them to libraries.

Certification. The action taken by a legally authorized state body on the professional or technical qualifications of librarians and library workers in publicly supported libraries, based on standards adopted by the body or similar action on a voluntary basis by a professional group, such as a state library association.

Charge Record. (File Material). In special libraries, a collection of material about associations, institutions, and other nonprofit organizations; e.g., annual reports, lists of officers and members, statements of purpose, list of publications, and other data on specific organizations.

Charging Department. (See Circulation Department.) 1. The part of a library from which books for outside use are lent regularly to adults and young people. 2. The administrative unit in charge of all the routines connected with lending books for outside use to adults and young people. Also called Delivery Department, Issuing Department, Lending Department, and Loan Department.

Charging File. A record of books loaned, usually consisting of book cards arranged by date or call number. Sometimes called Book Card File and Circulation File. A charging tray.

Circulating Library. A library that lends books for use outside the library. The term is now used almost exclusively for a commercial rental library. One of the small groups of books owned by a county school district and sent in rotation to the various schools of the district.

Circulation Department. The part of a library from which books for outside use are lent regularly to adults and young people. The administrative unit in charge of all the routines connected with lending books for outside use to adults and young people. Also called Delivery Department, Issuing Department, Loan Department.

Circulation Record. A record of books charged. Also called Loan Record, Statistics of the number of books charged daily for a given period. Also called Circulation Statistics. The record on a book card of the number of times the book has been borrowed.

Class Number. A number used to designate a specific division of a classification scheme whose notation consists wholly or in part of numerals. Also called Classification Number. The notation added to a book and to its entry in a catalog to show the class to which it belongs and indicate its location on the shelves of a library, in accordance with the classification scheme in use. Sometimes called the Class Mark.

Classification. A systematic scheme for the arrangement of books and other materials according to subject or form. The assigning of books to their proper places in a system of classification. In archives administration, the arrangement in logical order of the series of files within a record group or of the record groups within an archival collection.

Classification System. A particular scheme of classification, such as the Decimal Classification and the Library of Congress Classification.

Classroom Loan. A small collection of books, usually materials on a current school project, sent to a classroom for a limited period by a public or school library.

Collate. To ascertain, usually by examination of signatures, pages, leaves, and illustrations, whether or not a copy of a book is complete and perfect; also to compare it with descriptions of perfect or apparently perfect copies found in bibliographies. To compare minutely, page for page, and line for line, in order to determine whether or not two books are identical copies or variants.

Collective Biography. A work (or, collectively, works) consisting of separate accounts of the lives of a number of persons.

Consideration File. A current temporary file of titles suggested for purchase, consisting of order cards, publishers' notices, etc.

Continuation Order. A general direction to an agent or publisher to supply until otherwise notified; future members of a continuation as issued. Also called Standing Order.

Cooperative Book Selection. The policy adopted by two or more libraries of considering each other's holdings and selection of books before acquiring certain types of material or special items, in order to avoid duplication.

Cooperative Cataloging. The production of catalog entries through the joint action of several libraries in order to avoid duplication of effort. Particularly the plan by which cooperating libraries prepare copy for catalog cards to be printed by the Library of Congress.

Copy Number. 1. A figure used to distinguish copies of titles having the same call number or having no call number. 2. A number assigned to a particular copy of a book issued in a limited or special edition.

Copyright Date. The date of copyright as given in the book, as a rule on the back of the title page.

Cutter Number. An author number from one of the Cutter tables or from the *Cutter-Sanborn Three-Figure Alphabetic Table.*

Cutter-Sanborn Table. A three-figure alphabetical order scheme, an alteration for the two-figure Cutter table, made by Kate E. Sanborn. Also referred to as Author Table.

Date or Dating Slip. A strip of paper pasted on the inside cover or on the flyleaf of a book, on which is stamped date of issue or date when book is to be returned.

Decimal Classification. 1. The classification scheme for books devised by Melvil Dewey, which divides human knowledge into ten main classes, with further decimal division using a notation of numbers. 2. An earlier variety of classification based on shelf arrangement rather than subject matter, in which tiers and shelves, each numbered from one to ten, were allotted to certain subjects.

Demonstration Library. A library chosen or organized for an experimental purpose, in which a certain type of service is carried on during a specified period to prove the value of library service in the area.

Depository Library. A library legally designated to receive without charge copies of all or selected United States government publications; or a library designated to receive without charge a full set of Library of Congress printed cards.

Dictionary Catalog. A catalog, usually on cards, in which all the entries (author, title, subject, series, etc.) and their related reference are arranged together in one general alphabet. The subarrangement frequently varies from the strictly alphabetical.

Director of District Media Program. A media professional with appropriate certification and advanced managerial, administrative, and supervisory competencies who qualifies for an administrative or supervisory position.

District. A local basic administrative unit existing primarily to operate schools, public or nonpublic, or to contract for school services. A district may or may not be coterminous with the county, city, or town boundaries and may be identified by such terms as school system, basic administrative unit, local school system, basic administrative unit, local school system, or local education agency.

District Media Program. The media program that is conducted at the school district level through an administrative subunit.

Divided Catalog. A card catalog separated for convenience in use into two or more units, as, an author and title catalog and a subject catalog.

Division Library. A collection attached to, and administered by, a division or a group of related departments of a university or a college, usually with some form of cooperative arrangement with the general library or as a part of the library system.

Editor. One who prepares for publication a work or collection of work or articles not his own. The editorial labor may be limited to the preparation of the matter for the printer, or it may include supervision of the printing, revision (restitution), or elucidation of the text, and the addition of introduction, notes, and other critical matter.

Educational Technology. The broad application of scientific processes to the solution of educational problems and the fulfillment of learners.

Entry Word. The word by which an entry is arranged in a catalog or a biography, usually the first word of the heading. Also called Filing Word.

Exhibition Case. A glass-enclosed cabinet, sometimes built into a partition, or a showcase on a stand in which books or other material are placed for display. Also called Display Case.

Extension Library Service. The supplying of books and other library assistance to individuals or organizations outside a library's regular service area.

Fiction. In popular library usage, narrative prose literature, with events, characters, and scenes wholly, or partly the product of the imagination, as novels and short stories.

Filing Code. A body of rules for the systematic arrangement of cards in a catalog.

"First" Indention. The distance from the left edge of a catalog card at which, according to predetermined rules, the author heading begins; on a standard ruled card, at the first vertical line. Also called Outer Indention and Author Indention.

First-Word Entry. Entry made from the first word of a title not an article.

Form Card. A card used in catalogs that bears a printed or mimeographed statement applicable to many books, sets, headings, etc., with space for the addition of further information.

Full Cataloging. Cataloging that gives detailed bibliographical information in addition to the description essential for identifying books and locating them in a library.

General Reference. A blanket reference in a catalog to the kind of heading under which one may expect to find entries for materials on certain subjects or entries for particular kinds of names. Also called General Cross-Reference and Information Entry.

Hanging Indention. Specifically, a form of indention in cataloging in which the first line begins at author indention, and succeeding lines at title indention. (Ca.)

Head of School Media Program. A media specialist with managerial competencies, who is designated as responsible for the media program at the individual school level. Qualifications vary with such factors as the size of the school, size of media staff, and type of program.

Imprint. 1. The place and date of publication, and the name of the publisher or the printer (or sometimes both); ordinarily printed at the foot of the title page. Originally the term applied only to the printers imprint, which consists of his name and place of business. Later the term was extended to include the name of the publisher and the place and date of publication. The printer's name, with or without address, is now more often printed inconspicuously on the last page of the final signature. 2. The statement giving such information in a bibliographical description of printed work. (Ca.) 3. A book or other publication that has been printed. The term is often used for a book printed in a particular country or place, as "early American Imprint."

Indention. Specifically, the distance from the left edge of a catalog card at which, according to predetermined rules, the various parts of the description and their subsequent lines begin. (Ca.)

Instructional Design. The formulation and selection of management systems for instructional development.

Instructional System(s). An integrated group of program components organized to accomplish stated objectives.

Instructional Systems Components. All resources which can be designed, utilized, and combined in a systematic manner with the intent of achieving learning.

Instructional Technology. That part of educational technology concerned with applying scientific processes to learning experiences.

Interlibrary Loan. 1. A cooperative arrangement among libraries by which they may borrow material from each other. 2. A loan of library material by one library to another library.

Inventory. 1. A checking of the book collection of a library with the shelf-list record to discover books missing from shelves. 2. In archives administration, a list of the material in a record group arranged basically in the order in which the material is arranged.

Inverted Heading. A subject heading with the natural order of the words transposed, e.g., Psychology, Experimental. Also called Inverted Subject Heading.

Joint Author. A person who collaborates with one or more associates to produce a work in which the contribution of each is not separable from that of the others. (C)

Library Discount. Reduction from list price allowed to libraries by publishers, jobbers, local dealers, and other agents.

Library Instruction. Teaching readers how to use the library and make use of its materials.

Library of Congress Card. One of the printed catalog cards issued by the Library of Congress.

Library of Congress Classification. A system of classification for books developed by the Library of Congress for its collections. It has a notation of letters and figures which allows for expansion.

Library Planning. 1. Developing a plan for the design and construction of a library system. 2. The formulation of comprehensive integrated plans for library objectives in city, county, region, state, or nation.

Literature Search. Particularly in a special library, a systematic and exhaustive search for published material bearing on a specific problem or subject, with the preparation of abstracts for the use of the researcher; an intermediate stage between reference work and research, and to be differentiated from both.

Main Entry. A full catalog entry, usually the author entry, giving all the information necessary to the complete identification of a work. In a card catalog this entry bears also the tracing of all the other headings under which the work in question is entered in the catalog. The main entry, used as a master card, may bear in addition the tracing of related references and a record of other pertinent official data concerning the work. (Ca.)

Media Aide. A member of the media staff who performs clerical and secretarial tasks and assists as needed in the acquisition, maintenance, inventory, production, distribution, and utilization of materials and equipment.

Media Professional. Any media person, certificated or not, who qualifies by training and position to make professional judgments and to delineate and maintain media programs or program components. Media professionals may include media specialists, television or film producers, instructional developers, radio station managers, and technical processing (cataloging) specialists, whose duties and responsibilities are professional in nature.

Media Specialist. A person with appropriate certification and broad professional preparation, both in education and media, with competencies to carry out a media program. The media specialist is the basic media professional in the school program.

Media Support Personnel. All persons, including technicians and aides, who utilize specific skills and abilities to carry out program activities as delineated by professional staff members.

Media Technician. A member of the media staff with technical skills in such specialized areas as graphics production and display, information and materials processing, photographic production, operation and maintenance of audiovisual equipment, operation and maintenance of television equipment, and installation of systems components.

Microfilm. A negative or positive microphotograph on film. The term is usually applied to a sheet of film or to a long strip or roll of film, 16mm or 35mm wide, on which there is a series of microphotographs. (v) To make films.

Place of Publication. The city or town where the publishing house that issues a book is located.

Procedure Manual. A compilation of procedures for performing specific tasks or for fulfilling the duties of a particular position in a special library. It is usually more detailed than, but otherwise comparable with, the staff manual of a general library except for the elimination of personnel matters, which are usually contained, in the case of corporations, in the employee handbook.

Publication Date. 1. The year in which a book is published, generally the date given at the bottom of the title page, in distinction from copyright and other dates. Also known as Date of Publication. 2. The day of the month or week on which a periodical is issued. Also known as Publication Day. 3. The month and day when a new book is placed on sale by a publisher, generally announced in advance. Also known as Publication Day and Date of Publication.

Reading Shelves. Checking of shelves to see that books are in correct order. Also known as Revising Shelves and Shelf Reading.

Reference Collection. A collection of books and other materials in a library useful for supplying information, kept together for convenience and generally not allowed to circulate.

Region. A cooperative or legislated combination of districts.

Regional Catalog. A union catalog of libraries and collections

in a particular area which is responsible for collections in
a particular locality of section, such as a metropolitan
area, a state, or a group of states. Also called Regional
Union.

Regional Media Program. The program conducted by a region.

Reinforced Library Binding. A secondary binding in preli-
brary-bound style. (Properly used only to refer to Class A
prelibrary binding, but sometimes used in referring to a
prebound book in which the publisher's original cover is
retained.)

School. An organized group of learners under a professional
and administrative staff traditionally housed in a building
or adjacent buildings, usually part of a larger operational
unit.

School Media Center. An area or system of areas in the school
where a full range of information sources, associated
equipment, and services from media staff are accessible to
students, school personnel, and the school community.

School Media Program. The media program for a school, conducted through an administrative subunit.

Second Indention. The distance from the left edge of a catalog
card at which, according to predetermined rules, the title
normally begins; on a standard ruled card, at the second
vertical line. Also called Inner Indention, Title Indention,
and Paragraph Indention. (Ca.)

"See Also" Reference. A direction in a catalog from a term or
name under which entries are listed to another term or
name under which additional or all information may be
found.

"See" Reference. A direction in a catalog from a term or name
under which no entries are listed. Other terms used are:
"See" Cross-Reference, "See" Subject Reference, "See"
Card, and "See" Reference Card.

Serial Catalog. A public or an official catalog of serials in a library, with a record of the library's holdings.

Serial Entry. In a catalog, an entry, usually brief, of the several works in the library which belong to a series under the name of the series as a heading; in a bibliography, either a partial or a complete list of the works in a series. (Ca.)

Shelf List. A record of the books in a library arranged in the order in which they stand on the shelf.

Subject Analytic. An entry in a catalog under subject of a part of a work or of some article contained in a collection (volume of essays, serial, etc.), including a reference to the publications which contains the article or work entered. Also known as Subject Analytic Card, Subject Analytical, and Subject Analytical Entry.

Subject Bibliography. A list of material about a given subject, whether the subject be a person, place, or thing.

Title Analytic. An entry in a catalog under title for a part of a work or of some article contained in a collection (volume of essays, serial, etc.), including a reference of the publication which contains the article or work entered. Also known as Title Analytical Card, Title Analytical, and Title Analytical Entry.

Title Page. A page at the beginning of a book or work bearing its full title and usually, though not necessarily, the author's (editor's, etc.) name and the imprint. The leaf bearing the title page is commonly called the "title page" although properly called also the "title leaf." (C.)

In the case of works in the Oriental languages, the title page and the beginning of the text are normally at the back of the volume.

Tracing. In a card catalog, the record on the main entry card of all the additional headings under which the work is represented in the catalog. Also, the record on a main-entry card or on an authority card of all the related references made. The tracing may be on the face or on the back of the card, or on an accompanying card. (Ca.)

Union Catalog. 1. An author or subject catalog of all the books, or a selection of books, in a group of libraries, covering books in all fields, or limited by subject or type of material; generally established by cooperative effort. Also called Repertory Catalog and, sometimes, if on cards, Card Repertory. 2. A Library of Congress depository catalog combined with cards issued by other libraries, including, sometimes, cards prepared by the library with

the depository catalog. Sometimes called Union Depository Catalog. 3. A central catalog. (q.v.)

Unit Card. A basic catalog card, in the form of a main entry,
which when duplicated may be used as a unit for all other
entries for that work in the catalog by the addition of the
appropriate heading. Library of Congress printed cards
are the most commonly used unit cards. (C.)

Visible Index. 1. A series of metal frames or panels for holding card records so that a group of cards can be seen at
one time. Also called Visible File. 2. A record kept in such
a device, such as a list of serials, with or without holdings.

Withdrawal. The process of removing from library records all
entries for a book no longer in the library.

Word-by-word Alphabetizing or Alphabeting. Arranging alphabetically, with words rather than letters as units.

Notes

Selected terms taken mainly from *A.L.A. Glossary of Library Terms* (prepared under the Direction of the Committee on Library Terminology of the American Library Association by Elizabeth H. Thompson. Chicago: American
Library Association, 1943.

Webster's New Collegiate Dictionary, (Springfield, Mass.: G. & C. Merriam Company, 1976).

Index